THE LIVING CHURC

Christianity and Communism Today — *John C. Bennett*
The Church and the Arts — ed. *F. J. Glendenning*
Anglican Public Worship — *Colin Dunlop*
The English Religious Tradition — *Norman Sykes*
The Self in Pilgrimage—New Insights in Psychiatry and Religion — *Earl Loomis*
Experiments in Prayer — *Peter Coleman*
After the Apostles — *John Foster*
Ascent to the Cross — *Erik Routley*
The School of Prayer — *Olive Wyon*
Local Church and World Mission — *Douglas Webster*
Life Together — *Dietrich Bonhoeffer*
The Altar Fire — *Olive Wyon*
About Christ — *William Temple*
On the Move to Unity — ed. *J. E. Fison*
The Christian Ministry in Africa — *Bengt Sundkler*
The Family Is Not Broken — *G. R. Dunstan*
The Service of Our Lives — *J. E. T. Hough & R. W. Thomson*
A Future for the Free Churches? — *Christopher Driver*
A Calvin Treasury — intro. *T. F. Torrance*
Agenda for Anglicans — *Dewi Morgan*
The Biblical Doctrine of Work — *Alan Richardson*
A Conversation about Baptism — *R. L. Child*
Christ's Call to Service Now — ed. *Ambrose Reeves*
The Reformed Pastor — *Richard Baxter*
Christ's Strange Work — *Alec R. Vidler*
Windsor Sermons — *Alec R. Vidler*
The New Testament in Current Study — *R. H. Fuller*
Death and Life Have Contended — *H. A. Hodges*
Notebooks — *Florence Allshorn*
A Parish Priest Takes Stock — *A Parish Priest*
Last Things First — *Gordon Rupp*
The All-Sufficient Christ — *William Barclay*
A Conversation About the Holy Communion — intro. *Max Warren*
'Pro-Existence' Christian Voices in East Germany — ed. *Elizabeth Adler*
Servants of God in People's China — *Katharine Hockin*
The Question of Christian Stewardship — *James Mark*
The Greatest Old Testament Words — *Edgar Jones*
Key Words of the Gospel — *H. Berkhof & Philip Potter*

PREPARING FOR THE MINISTRY OF THE 1970s

Essays on the British Churches

by

H. G. G. HERKLOTS
JAMES WHYTE
ROBIN SHARP

edited by

DAVID L. EDWARDS

SCM PRESS LTD
BLOOMSBURY STREET LONDON

also edited by David L. Edwards

PRIESTS AND WORKERS
THE HONEST TO GOD DEBATE

First published 1964

Printed in Great Britain by
Charles Birchall and Sons Ltd
Liverpool and London

CONTENTS

PREFACE · 7

I · *The Church of England* · 11
H. G. G. HERKLOTS

II · *The Church of Scotland* · 89
JAMES WHYTE

III · *The Free Churches* · 109
ROBIN SHARP

PREFACE

THE ordained ministry in the Christian churches needs to be renewed. Everyone knows that, and sees that normally new training must come before new work. There is already a discussion about aims and methods active throughout the Christian world. It is commonly agreed that the ordained ministry is only a fraction of the total work of the Church, that the most important part of the new training required must concern the personal *discipleship* of the priest and minister, and that training must be continuous year by year *after* ordination. There is also a widespread ferment of debate about what might be called the more 'public' side of the work of the ordained ministry—that part of a parson's job which can be organized—and about the preparation of students for it. We seek to contribute to this debate.

Although the authors are alone responsible for its contents, the publication of this little book reflects the long established concern of the Student Christian Movement of Great Britain and Ireland for the lives and aspirations of those of its members who are to be ordained and for the effectiveness of the churches which they are to serve. A book might have been written about a spotless church which theological students, or prophets in their first pulpits, might imagine as flourishing in the 1980s—the Church of Utopia. Instead, the criticisms of the present situation which are here submitted or implied are all directed towards reforms which are 'practical politics', and the book is offered as a contribution towards a more serviceable ministry in the British churches in the immediate future. It is therefore hoped that not only theological students, but also responsible churchmen, lay or ordained, may be interested in it.

The main part has been written by Canon Hugh Herklots of Peterborough Cathedral, who is Moderator of the Church of England's 27 teacher-training colleges. He was invited to sum up his reflections because of his knowledge of the Christian mission in industrial England gained as Youth Secretary of the British Council of Churches, in the diocese of Sheffield and as Vicar of Doncaster, and because his practical experience of parochial realities is accompanied by an understanding of education, gained partly through his work training ordinands in St John's College, Winnipeg, before the war. The first draft of his contribution was ready before the publication of *The Deployment and Payment of the Clergy* by Mr Leslie Paul and *Clergy Training Today* by Canon Basil Moss, and about those other 1964 books by self-critical Anglicans Canon Herklots writes: 'In my revised pages I show that I am at least aware of them, but they have not caused me to change opinions previously formulated. Indeed I have been surprised to discover how much we are in agreement.' The SCM Press is much indebted to Canon Herklots, and to Bishop Craske and others associated with the Central Advisory Council for the Ministry, who generously helped his inquiry.

Professor James Whyte of the University of St Andrews, the next contributor, was formerly a parish minister in Edinburgh. He now teaches Practical Theology and is chairman of the Scottish Pastoral Association, an interdenominational fellowship of ministers, doctors, etc., which unfortunately has no equivalent in England (but an Institute of Religion and Medicine is now being formed in London). He gives us glimpses of the traditional Reformed understanding of the work of the ordained ministry—and also glimpses of the Church of Scotland's present deep concern for its mission to its nation.

Traditionally the English Free Churches have held many of the same views as the Church of Scotland. But they also have their own concerns, particularly in this time when many of their traditions are under pressure both from the movement for Christian unity and from the secularization of the country. The Reverend Robin Sharp, the youngest contributor, is a Methodist. As secretary of the Theological College Department of the SCM (and until recently also of the Renewal Group within the Methodist Church), he is able to put us in touch with some radical and constructive new thinking.

These three contributions, made from different churches and different generations, naturally differ in emphasis, and no artificial conclusion will be attempted here. But the three contributions do, I believe, converge to suggest a single vision of a renewed ministry. At any rate, this book is published in the hope that as we react to it, in private reflection or in group discussion, we may be helped to equip ourselves for the work to which God now calls us.

DAVID L. EDWARDS

I

The Church of England

H. G. G. HERKLOTS

1 · THE MINISTRY OF THE PEOPLE OF GOD

FEW events in history are more remarkable than the spread of Christianity in the early decades and the means by which it spread. After the crucifixion of Jesus the Jewish authorities must have been convinced that the trouble would soon die down. After all there had been others before him and they had amounted to nothing: this false Messiah was now crucified, dead and buried; and as for his followers there was not a man of importance among them. The Book of Acts is, of course, a Christian document, so that a critic of the faith is not likely to take at face value the story it unfolds. Nevertheless the attitude of bewilderment that it attributes to the Jewish authorities rings true. 'Now as they observed the boldness of Peter and John, and noted that they were untrained laymen, they began to wonder, then recognized them as former companions of Jesus' (Acts 4.13 N.E.B.). Among the followers of the crucified prophet who should by now have been discredited, there was a boldness, an effrontery even, which they could not easily account for nor explain away. Nor was the movement confined to Jerusalem. It pressed out along the trade routes and was soon to be encountered in many of the cities of the eastern Roman Empire. The eighteenth chapter of Acts, which records events which took place at Corinth around AD 51-53, tells how Priscilla and Aquila arrived there from Rome—and they were already Christians. Apollos came from Alexandria, and he also had been partially instructed in the Christian faith; though it was necessary for the humbler couple to take this intellectual in hand and expound the new way to him in greater detail. Then, 'finding that he wished to go across to Achaia, the brotherhood gave him their support, and wrote to the congregation there to make him welcome' (Acts 18.26, 27).

The picture that emerges from this and other passages is hardly that of professional missionaries at work, nor of the deployment of clerical manpower. Lay people were on the move, Christians going about their work like so many others in the mobile society of the first century; and wherever they went they told others of the good news which had revolutionized their lives. And, one way or another, whether in condemnation or acceptance, people took notice. The missionary journeys of Paul were so extensive and came to be so well reported that they have formed the picture of the spread of Christianity in the early decades for most instructed Christians in later days. It is not always remembered that numbers of men and women were associated with Paul in the great enterprise; not only those in the first rank, such as Barnabas and Silas and Timothy, but others whom he would recall as fellow-soldiers, fellow-slaves, fellow-prisoners. 'I commend to you Phoebe, a fellow-Christian who holds office in the congregation at Cenchreae. Give her, in the fellowship of Christ, a welcome worthy of God's people, and stand by her in any business in which she may need your help, for she has herself been a good friend to many, including myself.' This is the opening of the sixteenth chapter of the Epistle to the Romans, which may well be read for the picture it gives of devoted church members in the first century. All sorts of people, known or unknown, were concerned in all sorts of ways; and in the presentation of the faith to the world outside everbody mattered. Paul could remind the Christians in Corinth that they were not important people, as most men reckoned importance: 'Few of you are men of wisdom, by any human standard; few are powerful or highly born. Yet to shame the wise, God has chosen what the world counts folly, and to shame what is strong,

God has chosen what the world counts weakness. He has chosen things low and contemptible, mere nothings, to overthrow the existing order' (I Cor. 1.27, 28). They might not look like revolutionaries. But that is what they were. And when, in the end, the forces of the state were summoned to crush the new movement, it was found to be strangely resistant. 'We are men of yesterday', wrote Tertullian at the close of the second century, 'yet we have filled all your places of resort—cities, lodging-houses, villages, towns, markets, even the camp, tribes, town-councils, palace, senate, forum; we have left you nothing but your temples.'[1]

'We cannot hesitate to believe that the great mission of Christianity was in reality accomplished by informal missionaries', wrote Harnack in *The Expansion of Christianity*.[2] 'Justin says so explicitly. What won him over was the impression made by the moral life which he found among Christians in general. . . . We may safely assume, too, that women played a leading role in the spread of this religion.' It may be hazarded that the faith spread for three reasons. First was the message proclaimed by the evangelists of a God who had visited and redeemed his people—indeed *all* people if they would but accept it. Second was the corporate life of the little societies of men and women who had accepted this message as true. Third was the moral power expressed in their lives. These people had courage. They were not afraid of death. Men and women attracted others to the faith by the results of that faith in their own lives, by being what they were. To the Corinthian Christians, whose social origins were base, and whose behaviour was often at fault, Paul could write, 'Now you are Christ's body, and each one of you a limb or organ of it' (I Cor. 12.27).

Within the ministry of the whole Church there quickly emerged a diversified ministry of those with special gifts. The passage from I Corinthians continues, 'Within our community God has appointed, in the first place apostles, in the

[1]*Apol.* 37. [2](Williams and Norgate, 1904), vol. I, p. 460.

second place prophets, thirdly teachers; then miracle-workers, then those who have gifts of healing, or ability to help others of power to guide them, or the gift of ecstatic utterance of various kinds. Are all apostles? all prophets? all teachers? Do all work miracles? Have all gifts of healing? Do all speak in tongues of ecstasy? Can all interpret them? The higher gifts are those you should aim at.' Local churches cannot have been very large. If most of these gifts were to be looked for in any one church there must have been a clear sense of commitment, of everyone contributing, of everyone belonging and belonging to one another. It was as the people of God, the Israel of God that the Church lived its life, and served its Master, and won its converts. Nor was the apostle Paul separated off as what we might call a 'full-time employee of the Church'; for it was at Corinth that 'he fell in with a Jew named Aquila, a native of Pontus, and his wife Priscilla; he had recently arrived from Italy because Claudius had issued an edict that all Jews should leave Rome. Paul approached them and, because he was of the same trade, he made his home with them, and they carried on business together; they were tent-makers' (Acts 18.1-3).

In time those who were recognized as successors of the apostles became more important and their ministry more professional. Certainly this was the situation in the fourth century, after the Emperor Constantine had accepted the Christian faith. A primitive diversity of Christian institutions had become more standardized. The Middle Ages were to witness an efflorescence of orders and sub-orders, and of orders in the other sense of the different forms of monasticism. In the earlier Middle Ages a high proportion of those who could read or write were in orders of some kind: some in the direct service of the Church, others in the more secular employment of service to lord or king. To draw a sharp distinction between Church and State would be an anachronism: the two were different aspects of one Christian society. Yet the sense of the Church as the people of God was being lost; partly, indeed, because most men knew their weaknesses and had few illusions about themselves; partly because those outside the Church were rare or distant. The Prayer Book's Good Friday collect for Jews, Turks, Infidels and Hereticks is drawn from an earlier source. These were the categories of those outside the Church as they were known to believers in the Middle Ages and at the time of the Reformation—and all were foreign or strange. By Shakespeare's time to be a churchman meant to be in orders[1]—the heresy that to 'go into the Church' is to be ordained is not new. And it may be claimed that the effect of the Reformation, unintentional indeed, was to make the ministry even more professional than it had been before, more separated from the ordinary life of men. 'The avowed aim of the Protestant reformers', Dr F. R. Barry has written, 'was to set religion free from the cloister, to deliver it from its monastic exclusiveness, to establish Christian faith and piety as the inspiration of the home and the market-place. But in fact the results of the reforming movement have worked in almost the opposite sense. The tendency ever since the Reformation, both in the Roman and the Reformed Churches, has been to think of religion in isolation, as a self-sufficient and self-sustaining activity.'[2] If this has been true of religion as a whole—and the recent demand for a 'religionless Christianity' is evidence of it—within the life of the Churches the professional ministry has been contracted yet more narrowly. These are the men who are responsible, who run things, who seem indispensable.

But what happens when the indispensable has to be dispensed with? That occurred in a number of situations during the war and it is a condition which may almost be described as endemic in parts of Asia and Africa. Yet in the course of adaptation to circumstances—remembering that the leading of the Holy Spirit may be found in the challenge those circumstances present—a healthier way of life and a deeper understanding of the gospel may be found. In his

[1] Cf. *Twelfth Night*, Act III, Scene I.
[2] *The Relevance of Christianity* (Nisbet, 1932), p. 23.

war-time tract *The Wretchedness and Greatness of the Church,*[1] Dr W. A. Visser 't Hooft, then Secretary of the World Council of Churches 'in process of formation', wrote of the re-discovery of the Bible in many countries. A re-discovery of the Bible brought with it a re-discovery of the Church as the Body of Christ. 'It is striking to notice how large a part of this Bible study is led by the laity.... Today there are hundreds of parishes in Europe whose pastor is in a concentration camp, in a prisoner-of-war camp, or at the front. But these parishes are none the less *alive*. The ordinary members of the parish preach, administer the sacraments, teach the catechumens, visit the people. And the parish does not suffer. On the contrary, it renews its life.... We must free ourselves from the prejudice that this grace of the diversity of ministries and of the mobilization of the whole parish is granted only as an exception.... We must refuse to accept the present decadence of the Church and the disappearance of the gift of the diversity of ministries it once received.'

When the ten formative years of the World Council of Churches ended with its constitution at the first Assembly at Amsterdam in 1948 a concern for the laity in the Church had remained. And it still remains. There is now a World Council of Churches Department on the Laity; and at the end of 1960 its Secretary was reporting the preparation of an ecumenical bibliography on the role of the laity, containing 1,300 items. Many more must have been added since. Yet this is not mere verbiage. From this enquiry a fresh understanding is emerging. As Hans-Ruedi Weber puts it: 'The laity are not helpers of the clergy, so that the clergy can do their job; but the clergy are helpers of the whole people of God, so that the laity can be the Church.' This understanding, like so many other things, may be discovered latent in the Book of Common Prayer. We have already referred to one of the Good Friday collects. Another offers prayer 'for all estates of men in thy holy Church, that every member of the same, in his

[1](SCM Press, 1944), p. 38 f.

vocation and ministry, may truly and godly serve thee....'

It is within the total ministry of the people of God that the organized and professional ministry of the Church must find its place. This calls for new thought. There have been, and are, Churches whose whole ministry is voluntary. There have been, and are, lay movements within the Churches by which their life has been invigorated and their vision made more clear. The ecumenical movement owes much to these. There is now needed a fresh examination of the relationship between the different estates of men in Christ's Church. This will not be brought about mainly by study, at least not in the first place, but mainly by experiment, by trial and error. We have indeed been reminded by Hans-Ruedi Weber that 'the origin and context of the ecumenical re-affirmation of the ministry of the laity is not in the first place to be found in academic theology and official church gatherings, but rather in pioneering ventures where the Church meets the world'. Sometimes it appears that in this matter Anglicans have most to learn—and most to unlearn. The traditional education of Anglican clergy has often educated them *away* from their people rather than towards them; and the tradition of 'a gentleman in every parish' has often implied that the gentleman should also be the chairman; that he or his wife should be the prime mover in every parish, who gets things done—or prevents rash things from being done. At a higher level it seems generally assumed that almost every central board of the Church should have a Bishop in the chair.

Archbishop Temple once wrote: 'There can be no widespread evangelization of England unless the work is undertaken by the lay people of the Church.... The main duty of the clergy must be to train the lay members of the congregation in their work of witness.'[1] We might not express it in quite that way today; for there are not the trainers on the one hand and the trainees on the other. Clergy who think so render themselves unfit to understand those branches of

[1]Quoted in *Towards the Conversion of England* (Church Assembly, 1945), p. 36.

the Anglican Communion where the laity plays its part in synodical self-government, or the role of elder in Churches of the Reformed tradition. The process of training is at least one of mutual interaction, as laity and clergy together discover what it might be to be the Church effective in the world, like salt, or like light.

The secular world itself is not waiting to be taught or trained. The Church must win again its right to be heard; and this will not be achieved in the first place either by persuasiveness of speech or by skill in using means of communication made available by a technical age. The world needs to see the Church in the form of a servant; and that is what ministry means. 'The Son of man did not come to have servants but to be a servant' is the Basic English translation of Mark 10.45. 'It is not ourselves that we proclaim,' wrote Paul to the Corinthians (II Cor. 4.5), 'we proclaim Christ Jesus as Lord, and ourselves as your servants, for Jesus' sake.' This should be the ministry of the whole Church to those outside; and service must often go before proclamation—not talking about service but being occupied in it. There is a ministry of act which may prepare the way for the ministry of the Word and Sacraments—and which must be continued, for Jesus' sake, whether it prepare that way or not. In the ministry of the Church there are those specially chosen for particular functions. But the Church's relationship to the world must itself be one of increasing ministry; the ministry of the people of God.

2 · FOR GRANDPARENTS OR GRANDCHILDREN?

'*Some of us are more concerned about the Church of our grandchildren than the Church of our grandparents.*' So wrote a Methodist Minister in the *Guardian*,[1] controverting another who had been critical of the Report on Con-

[1] 6th March, 1963.

versations between the Church of England and the Methodist Church. His attitude will be shared by many. The Church must look forward. Yet it must also look back. *Remember!* is one of the watchwords of the Scriptures. The phrase 'from generation to generation' is another. The Hebrews looked back before they looked forwards. The first evangelists announced as part of their Good News that earlier promises had been fulfilled. From the pages of the New Testament there springs an urgent sense of the importance of the present; a 'now' in which decision must be made. How is this New Testament 'now' to be made really now in the latter half of the twentieth century? The forms of our religion reach back to what for most worshippers must be a distant past. The Book of Common Prayer is mostly four hundred years old; and a great proportion of what it contains is an English version of what had first appeared in other languages many centuries earlier. *As it was in the beginning, is now, and ever shall be* might appear to be the guiding principle. In the theological college at Cuddesdon near Oxford there was a time when the words 'keep the deposit'—printed in the original Greek of I Tim. 6.20 even on the crockery—were repeated so often by the saintly Principal, Edward King, that they were assumed to be the original motto given to the College by its founder Bishop Wilberforce.[1]

A tension between old and new belongs to the nature of religion; and it is at the point of tension that the minister must live. A new religion would naturally be suspect; yet a living faith is perpetually made new. It has often been thought that the task before the minister is to translate the gospel into modern terms. Translation is indeed important; and new translations of the Scriptures provide a valuable tool and an admirable stimulus to thought. But they are not to be used as a substitute for thinking. And the task is more fundamental than anything covered by the word trans-

[1]Owen Chadwick, *The Founding of Cuddesdon* (Oxford University Press, 1954), p. 120.

lation. It is not, wrote Richard Niebuhr, 'simply an affair of translating ancient ideas into modern language, but of wrestling with ultimate problems as they arise in contemporary forms.'[1] The difficulty presents itself acutely to those who teach in theological colleges; for the men whom they are helping to prepare for the ministry will in time be facing, not the contemporary situation of today but the unpredictable contemporary situation of twenty years ahead. To quote Dr Niebuhr again, they must somehow be prepared 'to remain faithful servants of the Church in the midst of cultural change and yet to change culturally so as to be true to the Church's purpose in new situations.'[2] The message and purpose of the Church *are* old; but there is something wrong when they are felt to be old-fashioned.

The fundamental theological documents which the teacher uses are largely the same as those which were used by his grandparents, though he may interpret them differently. The discoveries at Ras Shamra have not done away with a need to gain familiarity with the text of the Old Testament nor have the Dead Sea Scrolls taken the place of the New. Indeed a familiarity with the text of the Bible, newly discovered as a living Word, is for some the most valuable possession which as ministers they can trace back to their formal theological education; while a gift of scriptural understanding, interpretation and application may be what is most needed in a theological educator. During the nineteenth century C. J. Vaughan prepared more than four hundred men for the ministry; not at any theological college but by making them partners in his own ministry, first when he was Vicar of Doncaster, then Master of the Temple, and finally Dean of Llandaff, the whole period being from 1860 to 1897. What did he teach these men, who were proud to call themselves 'Vaughan's doves'? He sent them out visiting; and he expounded the Greek New Testament. In later years the

[1]H. Richard Niebuhr (with D. D. Williams and A. Gustafson) *The Purpose of the Church and Its Ministry* (New York, Harper and Brothers, 1956), p. 3. [2]*Ibid.*, p. 57.

medieval historian G. G. Coulton was to recall his days under Vaughan at Llandaff and compare his old teacher with St Bernard, who 'knew his Bible inside out; Luther and Bunyan knew it no better. . . . The Bible became bone of his bone and flesh of his flesh. Thus men noted that, when he spoke from the Bible, it was as if he were composing, and not repeating; as if the Holy Ghost were speaking directly from his mouth. Some men will still remember how the late Dean Vaughan was accustomed to read the Pauline epistles with a quiet depth of conviction, and an exact justice of emphasis born of lifelong study, which gave the impression that he himself was reasoning with the congregation in his own words, rather than rehearsing those of another.'[1] There could hardly be better preparation for service in the twentieth-century Church than to be so transported in spirit into the Church of the first century.

The theological college teacher has inevitably to emulate the 'scribe who hath been made a disciple to the Kingdom of heaven' who is 'like unto a man that is a householder, which bringeth forth from his treasure things new and old.' The old things may seem intimidating to students at first, especially if their previous education has been in science or through experience of practical affairs. The Old Testament lecturer discusses the eighth century before Christ, and even the New Testament lecturer a situation nearly two thousand years ago. Lectures on doctrine are linked with the conflict with heresy in the early centuries of the Christian era and with dogmatic restatement in the Confessions of the Reformation period. The lecturer on worship may spend much time on the modern liturgical movement; yet he must also turn to the springs and development of liturgical forms, to the *Didache* and Justin Martyr, the service books of Sarum and the Breviary of Cardinal Quignones. And there is Church History—not always such a cordial for drooping spirits as Bishop Lightfoot seems to have supposed.

[1] *Two Saints* (Cambridge, 1932), p. 16.

Yet to turn to the past is to turn also to the present—for the ultimate problems of the faith and of man's predicament remain the same. The industrial chaplain may encounter Arianism on the shop floor and the vicar Apollinarianism in the Parochial Church Council. He will recognize these things for what they are; though he would hardly be well advised to use traditional designations to describe them in discussion and controversy—for that might be to put others at a disadvantage; to encounter the criticism at once of 'talking down' and of failure to communicate. The eighth-century prophets were living in their own modern times, facing pressing issues which have their present-day counterparts. Nor have all the questions raised by the Reformation yet been decided. Every Christian believer and every church building is a product of history. We have nothing which we did not receive.

What has been received needs constantly to be sifted. Most clergy have encountered in their parishes the liturgical conservatism whose governing principle is 'what we've been used to'. But it is not the task of the theological colleges to prepare men for 'what we've been used to'—though it may well give them the stamina to endure what seems to them so old-fashioned and the respect to appreciate those whose ideas seem to them so wrong-headed. The conservatism is not on one side only. The priest can have his own anachronistic conservatism. The breakdown of clergy in their middle years is sometimes due to their expectation of a social position which is no longer granted by parishioners and which they themselves lack the financial means to support. Meanwhile the inessentials of Anglicanism are still exported overseas along with the essentials, while the accessories from the ecclesiastical furnishers, designed upon gothic lines approved long ago by the Cambridge Camden Society clutter up sanctuaries from land to land.

There is need for a fresh consideration of the meaning of tradition in the life of the Church; and a beginning of this has been made in the published report *Conversations between the Church of England and the Methodist Church.*[1] What elements are to be found in a tradition which 'should give the Church momentum rather than acting as an inertia from the past'? First and foremost, we are told, are the Holy Scriptures themselves. Next comes an appeal to primitive Christianity. Further than this, there is within the Church a 'continuous theological conversation, from the teaching of the early Fathers to modern biblical theology'. Of importance also are liturgies and hymns and the writings of godly men. The appeal to reason has transformed the conditions in which theologians work. The documents of faith can no longer be treated in isolation from the circumstances in which they originated or the Christian community from which they come. 'The appeal to history means the use of historical means of investigation, and a new sifting of non-theological factors at work in the history of the Church.'

It is with tradition, so interpreted, that the student in the theological college is confronted. He takes his part, timidly or brashly, within the continuing theological conversation. He may well agree that it is at this point that 'the tragedy of Christian divisions is most evident. Great Christian communities have been cut off from one another through many centuries and over large portions of the earth.' At this point, also, he may recall that what he has received from the past is received for use. He is heir to the past; but he must live in the present. He is aware of his grandparents; but may he not have grandchildren?

In thinking of this uncertain future at least six issues emerge to which thought must be given in training students for the ministry.

There is, first, the *ecumenical* issue. This century, so far as it has gone, has witnessed a remarkable coming together of the separated Churches, both on a world scale and locally. There is growth of understanding across the Catholic-Protestant gulf. The creation, in 1947, of the

[1]Church Information Office and the Epworth Press, 1963. See pp. 15 ff.

Church of South India, formed from Anglican, Congregationalist, Presbyterian and Methodist elements, has set a pattern likely to be followed elsewhere, even though with significant modifications. In Britain, despite set-backs, discussions between Anglicans and Presbyterians persist. Meanwhile the Conversations between the Church of England and the Methodist Church raise new hopes of reconciliation and union. 'Although the way to unity is sometimes dark, we are persuaded that we have travelled too far along the road ever to want to turn back. We are conscious of a divine compulsion mediated, as we believe, through a deeper insight into the abiding significance of the gospel, and a growing sensitiveness to the need of the world for the proclamation by the One Church of our common faith.'[1] Is this compulsion felt in the colleges? Or is there still what the Report calls elsewhere 'the compulsive narrowness of a denominational ethos' and 'a sterile and backward acceptance of an uncriticized inheritance'?[2] Students for the ministry must surely be trained in the hope of a coming unity. There is probably need for increased co-operative planning to ensure this. In the United States of America, we are told by the Director of the American Association of Theological Schools, 'most of the denominational schools accept considerable numbers of students from Churches other than their own. From within a short radius of the author's desk, for example—two Lutheran, one Disciples, one Evangelical United Brethren—count within their membership students from more than twenty-five denominations. Is this the Lord's way of preparing America for "the coming great Church"?'[3] How far would a development on these lines in Britain be possible—and how far would it be wise? The chorus would soon be raised that divisions are not to be overcome by pretending that they do not exist. Some entrants to theological colleges are well used to the ecumenical encounter; there are those, on the other hand, for whom it is at best novel and at worst outrageous. Yet they should not be allowed to

[1] *Ibid.*, p. 13. [2] *Ibid.*, p. 19. [3] *Expository Times*, Sept. 1962, p. 363.

remain enclosed in a self-satisfied Anglicanism, whatever may be the tradition of the parish from which they come. Meanwhile exchange visits between colleges of different Churches increase; and there is a growing feeling that the next theological college to be encouraged by the Church of England should be an ecumenical one.

Linked with the ecumenical issue is, secondly, the *international* one. In the twentieth century it has become clearer than ever that the Christian Church is open to all mankind—or that it has a very limited meaning indeed. In the past it was possible to think of a Christian West sending out missions to the non-Christian world beyond. Today the West can no longer be labelled Christian. The Church is present all over the world, though as a dispersed minority like the Jews in the time of Christ—and, indeed, ever since. 'Christendom is taking a new form', the Archbishop of Canterbury said in 1962. 'It is no longer to be identified with European civilization because the rifts between this civilization and Christianity have come to be so great. Rather is it something not Western or European but something belonging to every continent and striving to embody itself here, there and everywhere in the world in relation to many races and many forms of human culture.' Representatives of these many races are living in England; so that a priest may describe his inner London parish as 'an international transit camp' while another can summarize his parish of eight thousand in the North West of the country as having 'a varied and movable population—many in flats—all coloured—no sense of community—wild youth and indifferent.'[1] Nor is it unknown for a priest to be approached by the Muslims in his parish for the loan of a hall for the observance of Ramadan.

There are also many students from overseas in England and the numbers increase. Some are Christians; many are Muslims, Hindus or Buddhists, all of whose faiths have been

[1]These examples are from the 'clergy comments' quoted in the Report by Leslie Paul on *The Deployment and Payment of the Clergy* (Church Information Office, 1964), p. 63.

revitalized in modern times. Many are scientific humanists and many are attracted by Marxism. It is for a Church in this setting—whether in Britain or India—that students for the ministry are to be prepared; and theological colleges already welcome students and clergy from overseas. Those who go from England to Africa and Asia will already have learned that they go as servants of the Church in those lands. A world outlook is not the prerogative of those who have offered for service abroad; it needs to be shared by all who prepare for the ministry anywhere.

A third awareness that is needed is of the *architectural* setting of Christian worship and the form of buildings which are to provide a centre for the Christian enterprise. The church building has been usually taken for granted in the past. It should, where possible, be an old one; and if an old one were not available, one made to look old—even with the inconveniencies of the Middle Ages cunningly contrived by the ingenuity of gothic revivalists. At the Reformation the authorities of the Church of England found themselves in possession of buildings designed for a form of worship which the Reformers had repudiated. They did not really fit the Prayer Book. 'The Prayer Book conceives of each service in the liturgy as the work of the whole body of the faithful; medieval churches with their screens separating clergy and and laity, and the laity from the altar, tended to make the faithful largely onlookers and the liturgy the peculiar and exclusive work of the clergy.'[1] The Elizabethans turned altars into holy tables and transferred them to the body of the church. The seventeenth century high churchmen restored them to their old position, while the Oxford Movement in the nineteenth century restored the medieval emphasis. Today the movement is Elizabethan once more—and not in the Church of England alone. A *Guardian* reporter visiting the New Churches Exhibition at the Christian Art Centre, All Hallows on the Wall, London, in

[1]G. W. O. Addleshaw and Frederick Etchells, *The Architectural Setting of Anglican Worship* (Faber and Faber, 1948), p. 22.

March, 1963, concluded from an examination of the designs and models of twenty-six churches of different denominations that 'There seems to be no such thing as a rectangular place of worship today.' He found 'hexagonal, octagonal and ten-sided plans, as well as semi-hexagons linked to half-octagons and various amoeboid shapes.' These designs are not so much the product of fashion as of a desire to link priest and people round the altar. 'The task of the church architect is not merely to find a contemporary idiom. It is rather to create architectural forms which embody the theological vision of the twentieth century as the characteristic forms of Gothic architecture expressed those of the twelfth.'[1] The questions raised by this architecture are theological ones—to be discussed in theological colleges, however much the architectural setting of theological study, provided by the nineteenth century, may seem to hanker after the Middle Ages.

It is not the setting of worship only that needs to be considered but all the buildings which the Church uses. Are they in any way designed for witness? Where is the minister's room to be—and is it to be thought of primarily as a study or as an office or as a consulting-room? What provision should there be for classes and for social activities? Should the church buildings of the twentieth century be erected as solidly as those of the nineteenth, which are now, in some places, such an embarrassment? Are temporary buildings unworthy of a pilgrim people? In housing estates the church buildings are often described as a 'church centre'; and the designing of a church centre might well prove a valuable exercise in theological education. It would be a searching enquiry into the scale of values of those who would be the ministers of tomorrow.

The fourth issue is *intellectual*. Much could be written about this. It is not merely that the message and purpose of the Church must be thought out afresh in changing circum-

[1]Peter Hammond, *Liturgy and Architecture* (Barrie and Rockliff, 1960), p. 11.

stances: the nature of those changing circumstances needs itself to be grasped. The spread of education, of higher education in particular, has been on a revolutionary scale. African universities now stand where ten years ago there was nothing but the bush. The growth of universities in Britain seems rapid; but it is far slower than what is taking place elsewhere. There is needed a generation of clergy who can measure up to these needs and opportunities. For there is a danger, as they put it in Africa, that the pew may be above the pulpit. Bishop Sundkler quotes a South African Christian as saying, 'My school results drove home into me this idea that going into the ministry would be a waste of my intellectual capabilities.' A leading African layman from Sierra Leone declared, 'Brilliant students do not become pastors. Theology is for those who have failed to get an entrance into the secondary school.'[1]

The situation in England is, of course, different. But it is sometimes comparable. The intellectual standards for entry into a theological college are often lower than those required for a teacher-training college. They need to be higher rather than lower. At the Anglican Congress at Toronto Dr Alan Richardson made a telling quotation from Mr Christopher Dawson: 'The only part of Leviathan that is vulnerable is the brain, which is small in comparison with its vast and armoured bulk. If we could develop Christian higher education to a point at which it meets the attention of the average educated man in every field of thought, the situation would be radically changed.'[2]

Theological students need also to understand the nature of modern incredulity. There is hunger for belief also; as the sales of *Honest to God* give evidence. The questions there raised by the Bishop of Woolwich were familiar to theologians; what surprised them was that this particular exposure of the situation had so immediate and immense an appeal.

[1] *The Christian Ministry in Africa* (paperback ed. SCM Press, 1962), pp. 37, 41.

[2] *Anglican Congress* 1963 Report (SPCK, 1963), p. 167.

These questions are also discussed in every theological college. There may have been a time when theological students had to be *introduced* to the difficulties posed by their beliefs. Many today have felt those difficulties acutely themselves.

Dr F. R. Barry makes a good case for the policy of *back to the universities*. '1. If we are to have fewer men, they will have to be far better trained and qualified: for everybody will have to count for more than one. The clergy will have to be a *corps d'élite*. 2. The ordained ministry must be envisaged in the only context in which it makes sense—within the total ministry of the Church as the Body of Christ in the world. The clergy in future will have to be leaders and overseers of this corporate and mainly lay leadership. That is going to give them a new status and rescue them from being "odd men out". But this again means that they must be better trained. The evocation and nurturing of lay ministries will depend on the quality of the ordained ministry. If the latter is weak the former will not be there, and the Church will become more clerical than ever.'[1]

If the argument in the first chapter is valid, the clergy are not called to be overseers only. Sometimes they must accept oversight by others, being willing to take a subordinate place within the Church's mission. There is room for the man with ten talents, room also for the single talent *well employed*. Of such have been the saints; and it is saintliness, more than anything else, which impresses the man outside the Church.

A *fifth* change to be anticipated is administrative. The Paul Report calls for a new pastoral strategy 'in the light of the considerable social changes transforming England. As late as the outbreak of the Second World War, England seemed still a strong, even rigidly traditional society in which the class and role of a citizen at death was largely determined by his class at birth and the social milieu and schooling of his childhood. It is a socially fluid society to which a tradition-

[1]*Expository Times*, Nov. 1962, p. 43.

ally inflexible church organization, fashioned for more stable times, has now to adapt itself.'[1] This adaptation is already causing the status of the clergyman to be changed 'from that of the self-employed man with an independent income to that of the salaried servant of the Church.'[2] The conception, however, that the clergy should be *deployed* is still a novel one. 'Schoolteachers', Mr Paul points out, 'are distributed roughly in ratio to the population, though often with difficulty. When the population increases in an area, new schools are built and teachers recruited: when it declines, schools are closed and teachers sent elsewhere.'[3] With the ministry of the Church it is very different. 'The inevitable effect of the parochial system of deployment is at present to place most of the parsons in the country while most of the population lives in the towns.'[4] The Province of York is also served more meagrely than that of Canterbury.

The situation must therefore be taken in hand. 'Though the difficulties stare us in the face', writes Mr Paul, 'the alternatives are chilling—to do nothing, which means to abandon the nation to its religious decline and the clergy to their isolation, or to attempt a few piecemeal reforms which may save face but leave the central missionary problem to the conurbations unresolved. The crux of the whole problem of deployment seems to me to be this—though short of manpower the Church cannot use the clergy it has as effectively as it ought to do: it is a bad steward. It needs more clergy, but it has no moral right to ask for them unless it can deploy them more effectively. It cannot, one would have thought, remain content with what is virtually the self-deployment of the clergy upon an archaic pattern.'[5]

Administrative action is therefore proposed; that most attractive to the recruit for the ministry is probably the creation of major parishes, staffed by 'a college of clergy of which all members except those under training would have equal rights.'[6] Nor will any clergy be allowed to settle

[1] *Op. cit.*, p. 53. [2] *Ibid.*, p. 118 [3] *Ibid.*, p. 22.
[4] *Ibid.*, p. 23. [5] *Ibid.*, p. 171. [6] *Ibid.*, p. 176.

in a parish for ever: a ten years' 'leasehold' of a benefice could be renewed for five years but for no more. Equitable salary scales are proposed and an open system of promotion. It should be a condition of grant aid for training that an ordinand should accept direction for five years.[1] This might be more easily achieved if fewer ordinands were married or engaged to be married. The statement that 'It would be pastorally most valuable if young men entering the ministry regarded their first five years as "the celibate years" in gift to the ministry at the point of greatest need and delayed marriage till afterwards'[2] is not entirely realistic.

At the time of writing it is impossible to say how far this 'blueprint for the reconstruction of the ministry' will be carried out. But it is clear that the administrative pattern of the Church in the seventies is likely to be considerably different from what it is today. Yet a lover of tradition may hope that there will be a few anomalies left. It is, after all, a very western form of reconstruction which is being proposed—inevitably and rightly so. There must always be room in the ministry for the man called to a special form of obedience which no pattern of administration can envisage or, indeed, prevent.

The *sixth* issue which must concern the Church of the future will be that of mission, to which we now turn.

3 · FROM PARISH TO MISSION

In the development of the Church overseas there has often come a point at which the emphasis has changed from that of missionary work, supported and directed by a 'sending' Church elsewhere, to that of a settled, self-governing Church. In the nineteenth century there was talk of the '*euthanasia* of a Mission' which takes place 'when a missionary, surrounded by well-trained Native congregations under Native

[1] *Ibid.*, p. 172. [2] *Ibid.*, p. 182.

Pastors, is able to resign all pastoral work into their hands, and gradually relax his superintendence over the pastors themselves, till it insensibly ceases; and so the Mission passes into a settled Christian community.'[1] This has happened in many countries. In England, however, an opposite tendency is needed today. The settled Christian community, so far as it exists, needs to become unsettled; to be reorganized as a missionary force. It is not enough to be concerned for maintenance and repair. The Church is not self-perpetuating.

Two elements in the task of the ministry have been constant through many generations. In the first place it has been *pastoral*, and in the second *parochial*. The pastoral relationship—derived, it is to be recalled, from that of a shepherd caring for his flock—has been the special glory of Christian life in many lands. 'The work of a shepherd of souls,' writes C. W. Ranson in *The Christian Minister in India*,[2] 'is distinctively Christian. Other great religions have their prophets and teachers, their priests and administrators. The pastoral office, as exercised by the Christian minister, is unique.' More than ninety years ago, preaching at an ordination in St Paul's Cathedral, Dean Church used a tremendous sentence to elaborate the same point: 'The idea of a great ministry of reconciliation, with all its subsidiary ministries and stewardships and offices, the idea of a distinct use of human life, devoted, as to its governing and engrossing object, to a perpetual aggression against human ignorance and human sin—of an occupation as definite and as binding as a soldier's, in which teaching, comforting, warning, elevating human souls, shall have the place of the ordinary pursuits of life—of a call and mission, which set before a man as his appointed work in the world the communication to all whom he could reach, of the grace, and truth, and peace of Christ—this, one of the new gifts of

[1] A Minute of 1851, quoted Eugene Stock, *History of the Church Missionary Society*, Vol. II (1899), p. 415.
[2] (United Society for Christian Literature, 1945), p. 29.

Pentecost, came into the world first with the Christian Apostles.'[1]

If this be true, the pastoral ministry is a gift to be accepted humbly by the minister; a gift to be understood and so to be used that its value grows with use.

In the Church of England the pastoral responsibility has not been congregational only but specifically related to the inhabitants of a geographical area defined as a parish. The whole country is divided into these parishes, and, in theory, there is no person living in the country for whom there is not some priest who has a pastoral responsibility. The English parish is, of course, a venerable institution. 'Even today it is often possible, by following the line of a parish boundary, to trace the outline of an Anglo-Saxon estate as it is recorded in a tenth-century charter.'[2] Historians once derived the parochial system in England from the energetic administration of the great seventh-century Archbishop of Canterbury, Theodore of Tarsus; but it is now known to have been a slow growth—indeed it retained elements inherited from an earlier time before the English invaders crossed the North Sea. Patronage rights, which enable certain owners of property to appoint the local clergy, are ultimately derived from the relationship of landlord to priest in pre-Christian times. In England, as on the Continent of Europe, the words *parish* and *diocese* were in early centuries interchangeable. 'Only from the ninth century onwards, did parish and diocese begin to be used exclusively in the modern way.'[3] A Church organized primarily for mission was not organized parochially as it is today.

The parochial system developed as the needs of mission fell into the background. Its very rigidity implies that the fluid mission situation had ended and that the country was committed to the Christian faith. This was the assumption

[1] *Human Life and Its Conditions* (Macmillan, 1878), p. 126.

[2] D. M. Stenton, *English Society in the Early Middle Ages* (Penguin Books, 1951), p. 209.

[3] G. W. O. Addleshaw, *The Beginning of the Parochial System* (St Anthony's Press, n.d.), p. 7.

of the Book of Common Prayer, whose rubrics are designed for parishes small enough in population for every inhabitant to be known personally by the priest. Yet the modern assumption that only through the parochial system can the Church operate effectively appears to be historically false.

Needless to say, the pastoral ministry, in its parochial form, is too valuable to be lightly discarded. Its survival emphasises its power. It can still draw in many who have been too readily allowed to remain on the 'fringe' of the Church, as stewardship campaigns have testified. But it is more obviously fitted to a static society than to the mobile society which is modern England. To meet a missionary situation it needs, at the least, to be adapted and supplemented. It has been the hope of teachers in theological colleges to send those they have trained into 'good parishes' where their training will be continued and their devotional life sustained. But what will be the 'good parishes' of the future? Will they not be thought of as effective centres of mission?

Were a fresh start to be made much would be carried over of value from the past, though much would also be discarded. The Primates and Metropolitans of the Anglican Communion presented the Anglican Congress at Toronto in 1963 with a document entitled *Mutual Responsibility and Interdependence in the Body of Christ* in which they called for a new set of priorities on a world scale, and gave the warning that such a programme as they proposed 'if it is seen in its true size and accepted, will mean the death of much that is familiar about our churches now. It will mean radical change in our priorities—even leading us to share with others at least as much as we spend on ourselves. It means the death of old isolations and inherited attitudes. It means a willingness to forgo many desirable things, in every church.' These words are to be taken seriously.

When George Augustus Selwyn was appointed first Bishop of New Zealand he found that a new start *was* possible; and the clarity of his vision has significance for the present day. At his second Synod in 1847 he declared, 'The experience of a new colony convinces me that the Church of England system fully worked—

1. Under an able and pious head;
2. With sufficient clergy of one mind;
3. With no pecuniary bias;
4. With no State interference;
5. With free power of expansion;
   a. In its own field,
   b. Over the heathen world;
6. With a '*sacramentum*' of obedience;
   "Here am I, send me;"
   "I go, sir;"
   as well understood as in the army and navy;
7. With a definition of the duties of
   Bishops,
   Archdeacons, Rural Deans,
   Priests,
   Deacons, Schoolmasters,
   Clergymen's wives;
8. With an exclusion of all interference of relations as in the military and naval services:

That, these postulates granted, the Church of England would speedily become a praise upon the earth.'[1] The military analogy might not be approved by all; and the idea of a 'definition' of the duties of clergymen's wives might well be repudiated—but does not this list suggest ways in which the parochial ministry might be adapted in the England of the future? Indeed it is closely related to many of the recommendations of the Paul Report.

Another definition, from a recent investigation, indicates that the concept of a mission centre has dangers as well as attractiveness. Dr Abrecht has written: 'The mission station or compound was, in its day, a new form of society, a corporate structure of a kind absolutely different from any that had previously been encountered by Africans and Asians. It was a refuge for escaped slaves, for orphan children, for the independent spirits as well as the misfits of

[1]H. W. Tucker, *Memoir of the Life and Episcopate of George Augustus Selwyn, D.D.* (1879), Vol. I, p. 250.

tribal society. It was a state within a state, a system of law and order in situations where tribal rule had broken down and where colonial rule had not yet been realized. It was under the supervision of a Western missionary whose ideas about work and discipline were the rule and whose behaviour and that of his family inevitably became the pattern for all to emulate. It was controlled by a sense of order, and of the meaning of time which contrasted completely with the "native" world. Often more by accident than intent the missionaries and the Church were carriers of a new type of living and a new pattern of culture to people in these countries.'[1] There is much here that derives from the New Testament. When Paul wrote to the Philippians (3.20) that they were citizens of heaven he was writing to a small group in a city where the most important people were proud that they were citizens of Rome; and Paul's description was developed a few generations later by the unknown writer to Diognetus in his description of Christians who 'dwell each in his own country, but only as pilgrims and sojourners. They share the same duties as their fellow-citizens, yet suffer every indignity as foreigners. Every foreign land is, for them, a fatherland, and every fatherland is foreign. They are in the flesh but live not after the flesh. They obey the laws while passing their days on earth, but their citizenship is in heaven.'[2] Here, however, is not only a withdrawal from society but a permeation of society. There is in 'the Christian style of life', says the Bishop of Woolwich, 'an extraordinary combination of detachment and concern.'[3]

There is, inevitably, in Dr Abrecht's picture of the mission station something which derives, not from the New Testament, but from the old colonialism, from variants upon the British *raj*. A mission station of such a kind only remains possible in a decreasing number of countries. The pattern

[1] *The Churches and Rapid Social Change* (SCM Press, 1961), p. 24.
[2] (SPCK ed., 1943), p. 9.
[3] John A. T. Robinson, *On Being the Church in the World* (SCM Press, 1961), p. 18.

must everywhere be one of service, and though service be not recognized, or be misunderstood, it must still persist. The Body of Christ must be separated from the world, alien from it; yet at the same time implicated in the world, at home in it. The Western missionary becomes subordinate to others; becomes a real part of the Church in which and through which he serves. He has to learn another language; become at home in it. This is difficult for most English missionaries at work in Asia and Africa. It may be equally difficult for a minister posted to a mission station in England, working among people whose modes of thought and ways of expression are different from those to which he is accustomed and in which he has been trained. A writer on journalism has declared that 'The world observed from the offices of *The Times Literary Supplement* in Printing House Square differs a good deal from that seen from the shop floor of an engineering works in Sheffield, the cage of a pit in South Wales, the driving seat of an all-night truck on the Great North Road, the girls' rest room in a plastics factory on the Great West Road, the kitchen sink of a back-to-back house in Leeds, a dockside in Liverpool, or even a clerk's desk in an office in the City.'[1] It may be in language suitable to *The Times Literary Supplement* that most theological education goes forward, and rightly so; but in most of the situations described above its use would seem condescending and irrelevant, a manifestation of colonialism kept at home. 'To the weak I became weak, to win the weak', wrote Paul to the Corinthians (I Cor. 9.22). 'Indeed, I have become everything in turn to men of every sort, so that in one way or another I may save some.' Within the bounds of time the Church represents the eternal God; but it must do so after the manner not of transcendence but of incarnation.

The alienation of the industrial masses from the national Church—indeed, from any Church—has long been realized by those who know them. 'Church-going', it has been recently said, 'is uncommon except among the middle and

[1]Francis Williams, *Dangerous Estate* (Longmans Green, 1957), p. 288.

upper classes.... If, as luck has it, I am born in Camberley, there is quite a possibility that I shall end my life as a Christian. If, as luck has it, I am born in Camberwell, the possibility is remote.'[1] But, so long ago as 1904 Cosmo Gordon Lang, then Bishop of Stepney, was telling undergraduates at Cambridge: 'We are dealing with a people not lost to the Church, but waiting to be won.' (They are not nowadays waiting very expectantly.) 'They have not fallen from the Church, for they were never within it. No phrase could be more misleading than one which is often on men's lips—the lapsed masses.' It was found, he stated, in certain large centres of labour, that only one per cent of the workmen admitted that they belonged to any Christian body. 'It is a conclusion confirmed by my own experience. If you attend a gathering of working men in the East End of London on some political or social question, you can discern at a glance that they are a different sort of men altogether from those whom you meet in church or chapel.' Lang's lectures were published as *The Opportunity of the Church of England.*[2] The opportunity was hardly taken, not from lack of zeal, but from a failure adequately to diagnose the situation and to reorganize the resources of the Church to prepare for what such a diagnosis might reveal.

Church-going is uncommon except among the middle and upper classes. An invitation to church sometimes looks like an invitation to join these classes. The warning note from the mission compound needs to be recalled. It was so very different from the native world around. In the mission of Jesus there was indeed a separation of holiness between him and others; but there never seems to have been any separation of social class. What troubled his opponents was that he seemed to be so much at home among such disreputable people; he seemed to enjoy himself in their company so much. The mission of Jesus to the people of the land was not

[1]Eric James, *Odd Man Out? The Shape of the Ministry Today* (Hodder and Stoughton, 1962), pp. 29, 64.
[2](Longmans Green, 1905), pp. 39, 34.

to up-grade them to Pharisaic status. He was among them and they knew that he cared for them. Similarly, in the short-lived venture of the worker-priests in France it was the *presence* of the Church through them which made the deepest impression. They were there; and they cared.[1] This has been the secret also of the most effective parish work at all levels of society—for in the suburbs and in 'stockbrokers' country' men and women have souls and are sinners like the rest of us.

It is to be expected that in the coming decades the parochial system in England will be increasingly modified to meet the needs of a missionary situation. This will not be easy. It may involve giving up many things which seem important so that there may be a concentration upon what is more important still. Inevitably there will be further grouping of parishes—undertaken, it is to be hoped, not as a desperate expedient to meet pressing needs but as part of a plan. Of this the Paul Report offers hope. In some country districts the rural deanery may more often be the basic unit: within it there needs to be a careful integration of the varied ministries of clergy and laity. In towns there will not, it is to be hoped, be a division into more new parishes but an endeavour to strengthen effective church centres by supplying them with adequate staffs; again, of clergy and laity—men and women. This planning needs to be for a reasonably long period. It is important that there should be a staff; and just as important that the staff should stay. The work and witness of the Church is frustrated when a staff which has been built up and is at work is suddenly disintegrated because members have been lured away to posts elsewhere. The Church can probably make its best contribution in a mobile society more by stability than by mobility. Adaptability there must indeed be and much experiment; but the basis of adaptability and experiment needs to be reasonably secure.

[1]Cf. *Priests and Workers, an Anglo-French Discussion* edited by David L. Edwards (SCM Press, 1961).

The parochial ministry needs also to be supplemented. Three spheres of action come to mind. There is *first* that of industrial mission, which itself suggests the form of evangelism which may be most suited to our age. This is not a kind of commando raid into unknown territory, nor is it a fifth column placed there. The industrial chaplain goes in all honesty first to understand and then to share the concerns of men on the shop floor; only when he has done this can he begin to bring to those concerns an insight gained from his beliefs and from his discipleship. He starts where men are, and hopes that he may be able to help them to understand where they are better. Through discussion he may enable them to elucidate their own position and to see it in a wider frame of reference. When discussion is real, fundamental issues appear quickly, questions of man's origin, nature and destiny. His is a ministry of listening and sifting. So far as it is evangelistic it is, as the Archbishop of Canterbury has put it, through 'an evangelism which, at first, does not carry the gospel to men so much as get alongside them and help them in their feeling their way towards it'.[1] This is a lengthy process. Men are needed who will give themselves to the work and stay at it, being available, and, in the end, representing stability in a mobile situation.

There is, *secondly*, a similar ministry exercised by those who work from chaplaincy centres in the newer universities. For many decades the Church of England has shared in the work of the Student Christian Movement and of the Inter-Varsity Fellowship: many of its present leaders have served on their staffs or committees. Chaplaincy work, however, is comparatively new. There are now chaplaincy centres in all these universities. The pioneer work which is being done needs to be greatly extended. It is a recommendation of the Paul Report 'that the Church give highest priority to chaplaincies at the new universities and Colleges of Advanced Technology'.[2]

[1]Quoted in *The Task of the Church in Relation to Industry* (Church Information Office, 1959), p. 7. [2]*Op. cit.*, p. 210.

In the *third* place there is the work of chaplains and lecturers in divinity in the rapidly expanding teacher-training colleges; in particular, in the Church's Colleges for Teachers at which more than ten thousand students are now being trained for the profession. It might appear accidental that the Church has these 27 colleges, mostly inherited from a past when the Church was a pioneer in this field. It might also appear providential. As the result of past history the Church has now an opportunity to influence—but not to indoctrinate—a considerable cross-section of the young men and women of the country, who are themselves to influence many others. The chaplain is a kind of priest-worker; a worker, because it is as a lecturer that he has been appointed; and he must give of his best. But he is also a priest, a man set apart. He must *belong* to his college, being aware of what the students are talking about, what questions, presented by their studies or by the world outside are exercising their minds, who are their heroes and heroines, upon what issues a Christian judgment would appear to them to be relevant. Yet he must also stand apart as on behalf of the college and all its members he exercises the ministry of a priest.

There are many other specialized opportunities of service—chaplaincies in the forces, in hospitals, in the prison service, in boarding schools. If these varied opportunities are to be taken and used the process of training for the ministry becomes even more important. None of these opportunities can be used by those who have a cocksure temper. The member of a mission staff, the chaplain in industry or in education must never cease to be a learner. For specialized work men need to be carefully chosen; and the trainers of the ministry are naturally on the look-out for those of marked aptitude. But there is hardly as yet any effective means of recording and guiding these special aptitudes; it is all very much hit or miss. Some discover their particular bent after years of service, when they would welcome further training. The short courses which are common enough in this country are not enough. There is need for opportunities of much more prolonged second training, such as are open to clergy in the United States of America who may give up a succession of summers to qualify for a higher degree.[1] Industrial training in this country has made use of the 'sandwich course'—a return to college after a period out at work. The Church of England needs to do much more for its clergy on these lines if it is to meet its present missionary task.

4 · THE MINISTRY OF THE WORD

'Ye shall call upon them to hear sermons'—the admonition to godparents has been in the Baptism Service since the publication of the first Book of Common Prayer in 1549, though the opportunity to hear sermons may not have been very frequent in Tudor and Stuart times. The Injunctions of Queen Elizabeth I, issued in 1549, enjoined that parish clergy should 'preach in their own persons, once in every quarter of the year at the least, one sermon, being licensed specially thereunto, as is specified hereafter; or else shall read some homily prescribed to be used by the queen's authority every Sunday at the least, unless some other preacher sufficiently licensed, as hereafter, chance to come to the parish for the same purpose of preaching.' At the Hampton Court Conference, called by James I in 1604, the Puritans demanded a preaching ministry (at which Archbishop Bancroft interjected 'and a praying ministry too'. Richard Baxter, who was born in 1615, recalled his Shropshire boyhood, when the clergy were mostly 'readers' who never preached. The three or four 'constant competent preachers' who lived near 'were the common marks of the people's obloquy and reproach, and that any that had but gone to hear them, when he had no preaching at home, was made the derision of the vulgar rabble under the odious name of Puritan'.[2] In some parishes a benefactor might provide a way out of the diffi-

[1]This is a rather different suggestion from that of the Paul Report (p. 184) of at least *a sabbatical term*, away from parochial duties, for the clergyman in his early fifties. Both need to be considered.

[2]*Autobiography* (Everyman ed. Dent, 1931), p. 4.

culty by endowing a lectureship which supported an additional clergyman who preached; and there were other endowments for special sermons on particular dates. Later still, private enterprise—with an eye, sometimes, on the main chance—supplied proprietary chapels, where the sittings were bought up by eager hearers. Yet the complaint that the Church of England does not take preaching seriously is both old and persistent. 'Anglicanism', says Canon Howard A. Johnson of the Cathedral of St John the Divine in New York, 'hardly knows what a sermon is.'[1]

The Victorian age was none the less a great period of preaching—or, at least, a period of great preachers—in the Church of England as well as in the Free Churches; and the anxious provision of 'sittings' in the 'million pound churches' which were assisted by a parliamentary grant in the period after Waterloo, as well as by the rapid 'church extension' promoted by such as Bishop Wilberforce of Oxford and Bishop Fraser of Manchester, were designed to enable the populace to sit and listen as much as to kneel and pray. It was an age also of the published sermon. 'In its heyday', it has been said, 'the Victorian sermon, both as spoken address and as a literary production, performed some of the functions later assumed by serious weekly papers. It gave a *lead*....'[2] The sermons of the great also provided material for the sermons of the lesser. When C. J. Vaughan died in 1897 *The Times* wrote that 'his published sermons have afforded for many years an inexhaustible mine for clergymen too hardworked, or too diffident to compose their own discourses.' When one of the last of the great preachers, Hensley Henson, Bishop of Durham came in 1938 to make an anthology of sermons he could not but regret the passing of an ampler day. 'The congregations in all the churches and chapels in the country now form but a small fraction of the community. Sermons, unless they be reported in the news-

[1]*Global Odyssey* (Geoffrey Bles, 1963), p. 142.

[2]E. D. Mackarness, *The Heeded Voice, Studies in the Literary Status of the Anglican Sermon*, 1830-1900 (Cambridge: Heffer, 1959), p. xiv.

papers and are read by the people, appeal but to a petty minority. An educated public prefers articles in magazines to sermons in pulpits. It reads books, and newspapers, attends lectures, listens to orators on the wireless, but it has ceased for the most part to attend the churches. . . . The sermon which was formerly the most considerable element in the public service is being reduced in many churches to a petty feature. The traditional hour has been contracted to a few minutes. Great preaching is impossible in these circumstances. . . .'[1]

A petty feature for a petty minority; yet it is possible for something to be small but significant, not petty at all. At about the time that Henson was writing this *Introduction* the present writer happened to meet another great churchman—and great preacher—in the streets of Manchester, Canon Peter Green. 'I've just been asked by the BBC to speak for three minutes', he expostulated, 'and I've refused. It's an insult to the gospel.' Yet much can be said in three minutes; and the opportunity to speak about the Christian faith, though for three minutes only, to an audience numbered in millions, is not wholly to be despised. In succeeding decades the Church has learned much from broadcasting, and, not least, to make a significant point, or series of points, within an exactly apportioned time. The BBC also led the way in recording; so that a preacher could learn how his voice sounded and what were his more obvious faults. The discipline of taking these lessons to heart was painful but rewarding. Technical discovery does not stand still, and nowadays the tape recorder, once a novelty, is part of the equipment of most theological colleges.

'The most startling fact about the Anglican sermon,' wrote Archbishop Brillioth in 1949, 'remains the absence of a clear relation to the liturgy. That may find its explanation in the history of the worship. The Prayer Book of 1662, as well as those of 1549 and 1552, preserves the sermon in the mass, after the Creed and in connection with the

[1]*Selected English Sermons* (World's Classics, Oxford, 1939), pp. xii, xiii.

notices. But as the mass came to be chiefly the communion service, and gradually lost its place as the chief service of the day, the injunction to preach a sermon—or to read one of the homilies—fell into disuse. On the other hand, Morning Prayer and Evening Prayer became preaching services, although for them there is no provision made for a sermon in the order of the Prayer Book.'[1] In the years since Brillioth wrote the liturgical movement has made headway in the Church of England, particularly through the Parish Communion. This has called for brief and pointed utterance, short expositions of Scripture, teaching specifically related to the season, with its Epistle and Gospel. The very fact that this is the one service which many church members regularly attend has underlined the need for the introduction of Old Testament lections; so that the whole gospel may be preached, in its historical depth as well as in its immediacy.

'It is at Evensong that you are able to reach the outsiders.' This used to be said in the town parishes of the North of England. The opportunity is much more limited today; for at 6.30 p.m. families are settling down in front of the television screen or far from home in their own motor cars or on 'day trips' in motor coaches. If a public meeting is to succeed in these days the audience has to be 'packed', recruited in advance. It is not enough to make an announcement in the newspapers, to give out notices in church, to cover the hoardings with advertisements. A concentrated and persistent effort has to be made to bring people in. If the Church is to have anything in the way of a teaching mission the same imaginative persistence is required. Yet Sunday by Sunday the parson may preach in an evening to a dwindling few. It might possibly be wiser to forgo sermons at ordinary times and to concentrate on certain seasons for the presentation of the faith, such as Lent and Advent, when sermons can be consecutive, persuasive and challenging—with an opportunity provided for discussion afterwards. This would

[1] *Landmarks in the History of Preaching*, Donellan Lectures, Dublin, 1949 (SPCK, 1950), p. 38.

certainly be ineffective if it were but the desperate expedient of a despairing evangelist; it needs to have the congregation behind it; it must be an activity of the whole Church.

The candidate for the ministry, it appears, must be helped in advance to do three things. First, he will need to be able to give short addresses, few words of which are wasted, related to, and springing from, the ordered progression of the Christian year; talks which look out from the church building to the life of the world around and the daily choices which must be made by those who are linked in Christian worship. Yet though the congregation be swiftly dispersed it will be the endeavour of the speaker to show that its unity is not thereby impaired: the community of worship has become a community of witness and of service. Some, at least, should secondly be able to give more lengthy expositions, consecutive over a number of weeks, which will express and teach the faith, so far as possible in non-theological language, and with illustrations drawn from the life of the present. There is a necessary language of the theological specialist, expressed in terms which have little significance except for those who have been trained to apprehend their meaning and to discern their subtleties. But the language of religion is different. The great themes of the Bible are largely expressed in terms of basic human experiences and needs. The Bible speaks of birth and life and death, of light and darkness, day and night, of hunger and thirst and the food and drink by which they are satisfied, of sunshine and storm, of fire and water, of building and journeying and the city at the journey's end. Jesus, in particular, drew his illustrations from the life around him; the salt and leaven used in cooking, the good measure to be insisted upon at market, the garment needing a patch, the lost coin; outside the home were the fishermen and farmers, the shepherds and stewards and labourers in vineyards; and as he travelled with his disciples further afield there were the ditches by the roadside, perilous in the dark, the stumbling-blocks left by roadmakers who had not finished their job, the steep hillside, the narrow gate, and, no doubt, crosses outside city walls. 'Never be afraid to call upon your people to follow your best thought, if only it is really trying to lead them somewhere', said Bishop Phillips Brooks.[1] That thought will be more valuable to the speaker as well as to the listener if the former has followed the discipline of expressing it in simple terms, using exact images, rather than preachers' phrases which have become like pebbles worn smooth by innumerable tides.

A word often applied to preaching is the New Testament one, *kerygma*—proclamation. But there are many modern situations in which proclamation is hardly applicable. Sir Richard Acland has quoted the opening words of a discussion pamphlet issued by the Church Assembly in 1945: ' "Tell me the old, old story of unseen things above, of Jesus and His glory, of Jesus and His love." To do just that is, in essence, what the evangelist in any age sets out to do.' Sir Richard comments: 'Yes: the evangelists tell the people the simple and magnificent truth; and they *ought* to believe it —"just like that". But somehow they don't.

'Then what has gone wrong?

'What has gone wrong is that we have not taken sufficient account of the fact that our traditional method of proclamatory teaching is for the first time encountering a whole community whose minds are equipped with rough and ready tests by which they can separate the "almost obvious" from the "almost incredible".'[2]

The fact that many in that community are credulous does not alter the general situation. The Christian faith is being put to the test, not merely of ethical performance—of Christians 'living up' to the faith they profess—but of intellectual acceptability. This emphasizes the third ability needed today in one who is training for the ministry—that of being able to take part in a group discussion. The clergyman will often—too often—be asked to lead; but he should

[1] *Eight Lectures on Preaching* (SPCK, 1959), p. 113.
[2] *Nothing left to believe?* (Longmans Green, 1949), p. 17.

first discover in experience what a group is and what it can achieve through the contributions of its varied members. Here in a special way he must learn to be servant of all. He must learn to listen—and sometimes to be sensitive to the hidden anxiety or doubt which needs to be brought into the open. He will further learn to interpret, to express what others, perhaps, can only half express or what they hide behind many words. A larger knowledge may help him to show where thought has been inadequate, where conclusions have been too readily accepted, where questions remain to be examined and investigations need to be made. Yet he will come to recognize that there are many situations about which he is ignorant, many conditions about which he has no right to dogmatize; where the people of God, in their different vocations and ministries can only be learners together, learning indeed from one another as together they ask for the guidance of God and try to be obedient to his will.

This ministry of group discussion needs to be as carefully prepared for as a written sermon; prepared *for* rather than prepared, for there is no set conclusion to which dialectic must lead. It needs 'mastery of dialogue rather than monologue',[1] to use Canon Moss's succinct phrase. Whether the starting place be a passage of Scripture or an incident in contemporary life raising fundamental questions, it is the guidance of the Holy Spirit that the members of the group are asking for together. The weakness of many groups is that they lead nowhere. Corporate discussion can, however, lead to action more carefully envisaged and planned than exhortation from the pulpit; and action may become the basis for a further consideration of how God's Holy Spirit is leading his people forward.

Ye shall call upon them to hear sermons. The newly ordained minister will be called upon to preach them—though in the conditions of today he may not hear them very often. How shall he be prepared? Sermon classes in theo-

[1]Basil S. Moss, *Clergy Training Today* (SPCK, 1964), p. 24.

logical colleges have increased in number and in seriousness; but what they can do is comparatively limited. They can correct faults in utterance and indicate a necessary structure; but they can hardly impart the matter which is to be preached. What is needed especially is the beginnings of a disciplined study of Holy Scripture; and if it can be the beginnings of an understanding of the Scriptures in the original languages in which they were written, so much the better. Dr Cunliffe-Jones of the Congregational College at Manchester has written that 'The minimum requirement for all students in biblical languages should be: a knowledge of the Hebrew and Greek alphabets; a general knowledge of the main characteristics of the two languages; and a serious study of the main words of theological importance in both languages (without the rigour and discipline of accurate translation).'[1] There are clergy who could wish that at the beginning of their ministry there had been so wise and liberal an understanding of their needs. Modern translations and commentaries can do much. Yet there can be little doubt that the deepest and liveliest preaching—the preaching whose fount does not dry up—is given by those who go to the Old Testament in Hebrew and the New Testament in Greek. When more and more of the congregation have in their different ways to be experts and to accept the discipline of study an increasing number will respect the expertise of the preacher—provided that it is put to them in a way that invites their understanding. They are not likely to be helped greatly by what comes 'off the top'. 'Cases are won in chambers'—Dr J. H. Jowett[2] used to quote a barrister's words; then added, 'Men are not deeply influenced by extemporized thought. They are not carried along by a current of fluency which is ignorant where it is going. . . . Preaching that costs nothing accomplishes nothing. If the study is a lounge the pulpit will be an impertinence.'

[1]*Expository Times*, Oct. 1962.
[2]*The Preacher: His Life and Work* (Hodder and Stoughton, n.d.), p. 114.

Candidates for the ministry are given some help with their preaching when they are in college. The Bishops insist upon this; and it is clear that something of the art of communication may be taught. They may learn to look, as an artist or scientist learns to look; and to listen as a doctor listens. To be observant is a first step towards being able to communicate. It is in the parishes that they will be tested. They may be asked to speak too often. The tradition of expecting a 'few words' from the clergyman on most occasions when a group of church people meet is one that dies hard. When parishes were more strongly staffed the newly ordained deacon might be asked to preach no more than monthly: he heard other people's sermons; and the Vicar heard his. It can happen nowadays that the newly ordained deacon finds himself faced with the task of preaching on most Sundays in some mission church; with the result that he rarely hears his Vicar and his Vicar rarely hears him. Thus a time of training is denied. Faults go uncorrected and fluency is at a premium.

Throughout the course of his ministry, from start to finish, a preacher needs much help; from books and lectures, from the preaching of others, from criticism. He needs also to have a great conception of the task to which he is committed. He cannot patronize his congregation when he remembers that each one of them is a brother or sister for whom Christ has died. Nor can he underestimate his task when he considers its relationship to the living Word, the incarnation of God in Christ. A Swedish scholar, steeped in the Lutheran tradition, puts it in this way: 'The task the preacher faces is that of bringing about a meeting between the Word and men, of establishing a bond between the passage in the Bible and the congregation.' He goes on to state that 'in this meeting there comes about that for which both the Word and men were destined. *The Word* exists to be made known; only when it is preached is its objective content fully disclosed. Man was created in the beginning by the creative Word, and destined to live by that which comes from the mouth of God. Men understand themselves aright and receive true human life in the hearing of God's Word. The Word reaches the objective for which it was sent out only when it effects an entrance into men. Man reaches the spring out of which he can draw human life only when the Word of the Creator comes to him.'[1]

This is a high theology indeed; but it is not far removed from the language of the English Ordinal, when candidates for the priesthood are exhorted, in the name of our Lord Jesus Christ, to 'have in remembrance, unto how high a Dignity, and to how weighty an Office and Charge ye are called: that is to say, to be Messengers, Watchmen, and Stewards of the Lord, to teach, and to premonish, to feed and provide for the Lord's family; to seek for Christ's sheep that are dispersed abroad, and for his children who are in the midst of this naughty world, that they may be saved through Christ for ever.'

The thought is far wider than that of preaching alone. But in this wider ministry, pastoral and evangelistic, the preaching of the Word has a representative place, summoning the congregation into the presence of its Master; and sending its members out, on their several ways, through his guidance and in his strength to do his will.

5 · STEWARDS OF THE MYSTERIES OF GOD

The ministry for which a student is prepared is a ministry of the Word *and Sacraments*. The first time that the newly-ordained priest celebrates Holy Communion is likely to be for him a much more signal occasion than the preaching of his first sermon. He is now set apart from other men in a representative capacity which he holds for life, from which he can only be deprived for grievous sin; able to perform that liturgical action by which the life of the Church is

[1]Gustaf Wingren, *The Living Word, A Theological Study of Preaching and the Church* (SCM Press, 1960), p. 13. See also R. E. C. Browne, *The Ministry of the Word* (SCM Press, 1958); J.-J. von Allmen, *Preaching and Congregation* (Lutterworth Press, 1962).

maintained, and which constitutes its most vital link with the living Lord. 'The sacraments', wrote Canon Leonard Hodgson, 'are incidents in the social intercourse of God and men. As elements in that whole the water of Baptism and the bread and wine of the Eucharist, being instinct with God's redeeming purpose and our response, become charged with spiritual significance. As elements in that whole they are as different from water, bread and wine elsewhere as the atmospheric vibrations produced by a symphony are different from vibrations unregulated for the expression of purpose.'[1] In this social intercourse the priest has an essential part to play. He is as necessary as the water, bread and wine. His action, and his life as a whole, are also intended to be 'instinct with God's redeeming purpose' to which he responds both personally and on behalf of others. He has learned from the twenty-sixth of the Thirty-nine Articles that the unworthiness of ministers hinders not the effect of the Sacrament; and the nearer he draws to his Master the more acutely he is aware of that unworthiness. Yet he is not his own. His life has been given away. He must indeed 'magnify his office'; but it is a tragic failure when the priest uses his office to magnify himself.

At the Reformation there was a widespread rejection of 'priest-craft'. An accumulation of personal failure, expressing itself as personal self-importance encouraged this rejection as well as a belief in the priesthood of all believers. Some Churches also rejected episcopacy, partly because of an interpretation of early church history, partly because of an experience of the pretensions of prelacy. The history of the Anglican Communion sounds many warning notes, especially during that long period when the feeling of settlers in the American Colonies, encouraged by dissenters at home, saw to it that an episcopal Church must perforce persist without bishops. Many of the Churches which passed through the Reformation rejected priest-craft as an unwarrantable and dangerous interposition between the individual

[1] *Essays in Christian Philosophy* (Longmans Green, 1930), p. 110.

and God. Yet the Church of England held tenaciously to the three-fold ministry of bishops, priests and deacons; and its apologists were always ready to explain that the word priest is derived from the word presbyter, meaning elder. Priest-craft of some sort there must be. The priest is not expected to administer the sacraments amateurishly; and the penitent expects more than good-natured advice when he turns to the Minister of God's Word to 'open his grief; that by the ministry of God's holy Word he may receive the benefit of absolution, together with ghostly counsel and advice, to the quieting of his conscience, and avoiding of all scruple and doubtfulness'.[1]

The sacraments form the bond of a double relationship. First there is the relationship to God 'unto whom all hearts be open, all desires known, and from whom no secrets are hid'. Secondly there is the relationship to and within the people of God assembled in one place, all those who, in the Sacrament of Holy Communion, truly and earnestly repent of their sins, are in love and charity with their neighbours, and intend to lead a new life, following the commandments of God and walking in his holy ways. But there is also to be considered the bond itself, the action performed by priest —and by people—which unites them as a penitent, forgiven, receptive and thankful community. The Revised Catechism may define the outward and visible sign in Holy Communion as 'bread and wine given and received as the Lord commanded'; but *given and received* implies people. The Sacraments are incidents in a personal relationship with a living Lord; but also in the personal relationship of people with each other.

These three emphases are needed if a student is to be adequately prepared for his place in the Christian ministry.

A priest is called to be a man of God. Nothing could be more important in his training than contact with others who deserve that title. His life may already have been deepened by such an influence. Many a priest carries with

[1]Exhortation in the Service of Holy Communion.

him always the memory of the Vicar whose example suggested to him first of all a way he might follow; who encouraged and tested him; who 'fostered his vocation'. Nowadays this is by no means true of all. Many a candidate for the ministry—and we may be glad of it—is a comparative newcomer to Christianity itself; he does not remember the slow nurturing of a desire for the priesthood: he remembers his conversion and its consequences; a growing certainty that he must share with others what is good news for him. Yet by whatever route the student has reached a theological college the lives of the principal and members of the staff, and of his fellow-students, may all influence him deeply. When Bishop Taylor Smith was a student at St John's Hall, Highbury, he placed on his mantel-piece a card with the four words on it, 'As now, so then', to remind him that habits formed in College would endure into his ministerial life.[1] Cosmo Gordon Lang, throughout his ministry, would return to Cuddesdon, his theological college, for retreat and refreshment; and the principal could record the simplicity with which, even when Primate of All England, he would come. 'He was a son of the College coming home to the place where he had begun to learn his deepest lessons and glad to share its life once again.'[2]

In the English tradition of training for the ministry this intimate influence of person and place has been greatly esteemed. Theological colleges have not grown down from being departments of a University: they have grown up from being households around a principal and a tiny staff. The afternoon walk together of a student with his principal or vice-principal has been an occasion when difficulties have been discussed and opportunities assessed. A supreme example of this personal influence was that of Edward King, later Bishop of Lincoln, who was Chaplain of Cuddesdon

[1]G. C. B. Davies, *Men for the Ministry* (Hodder and Stoughton, 1963), p. 135.

[2]J. G. Lockhart, *Cosmo Gordon Lang* (Hodder and Stoughton, 1949), p. 387.

from 1858 to 1863 and Principal from 1863 to 1873. One who was trained by him later recorded, 'Until now we had never understood ourselves. At last the tangle was unravelled by one as familiar, it seemed, with every twist and turn as if he had himself lived it out along with us. Doctrine, sermon, meditation, each went home with direct personal application, until it was plain that our only course was to submit our lives and difficulties, our temptations and our sins, our hopes and fears, to one who seemed to know them all without needing to be told, and so benefit by the guidance for the future of one who had showed himself clairvoyant of the past.... The result was that men felt that they "owed their souls" to him.'[1] King also maintained contact with many of his former students after they had been ordained; letters of enquiry from many of them still followed him throughout the time that he was Bishop of Lincoln. In both these ways, as a personal influence and as a continuing adviser, he has been followed by others.

Yet there are dangers here, as in all forms of spiritual direction. In the ministry a man needs never to forget his fundamental dependence on God; but he should not be over dependent on any one of his fellows. The priest needs often to hear the words spoken to Ezekiel (2.1), 'Son of man, stand upon thy feet.' There are many situations in which he must take an independent line. The theological student may encounter in his training a depth of faith which he cannot but admire and wish to emulate; but his own faith must also be questioned so that it may become adult and secure. The mood of Robert Browning's *Bishop Blougram* should not be alien to him :

> 'With me, faith means perpetual unbelief
> Kept quiet, like the snake 'neath Michael's foot
> Who stands calm just because he feels it writhe.'

A man who has not had the experience of being shaken and upset by theological teaching in a university usually needs

[1]Owen Chadwick, *op. cit.*, p. 112.

something of the sort in his later training. It has sometimes been suggested that before young Christians leave the protected world of school they should be provided with answers to some of the disturbing questions they are likely to encounter. Model answers are often admirably put together; but the young person at his work may find that the questions are rather different from those which he had been led to expect and that the answers do not exactly fit. The man who enters the ministry of the Church does well to realize from the first that there are no ready-made answers to the problems and difficulties of life. But he may be able to help others if he has been through testing himself and found a way through. The author of the Epistle to the Hebrews (2.18) suggests that this is the very method of the Incarnation: 'For since he himself has passed through the test of suffering, he is able to help those who are meeting their test now.'

Awareness of holiness creates a desire for holiness. 'Lord, teach us to pray,' said the disciples to Jesus. He did not merely teach them a prayer, though he did this. He said, 'after this manner pray ye' (Matt. 6.9); and much of the truest devotional development in the life of the Church has been a working of this out. 'Teach us to pray' is the natural request of the theological student, and in replying 'After this manner pray ye' there is a natural turning to the Lord's Prayer, its meaning and its implications. Training in prayer is given through talks in chapel, and in the classroom, and in more intimate discussions with individual students. The planning of the day provides special opportunities to put the teaching into practice. The time of quiet in a student's own room or in chapel after corporate worship early in the morning is meant as much more than a training in self-discipline: it is intended as a first instalment of that great gift in a priest's life, an ability to turn from immediate concerns to the all-loving God, then to return to these concerns refreshed and with a new sense of proportion. But it is not always as simple as this. He will need to pray in circumstances that are difficult, where there is confusion and noise, but where the need for God's help is also very great.

In all this training the student for the ministry should encounter a sincerity of godliness which can mould his character and give direction to his life. This depends not upon the principal and staff alone; students learn much from each other. But he must also be professionally trained. He must gain some exact knowledge of those outward and representative actions which are the specific duties of a priest. If he has been a server at Holy Communion he may have some familiarity with these already; indeed he may be almost too familiar with them, too ready to discuss and appraise the niceties of liturgical accessories; too ready to make coy jokes about the way in which one priest celebrates and another takes the ablutions. At the theological college these things need to be put in their place. But if the sacraments are 'incidents in the social intercourse of God and men' there is room in their administration for a code of good manners. It is in his first curacy, rather than at the theological college, that the manner of administering the sacraments is to be learned in practice; though for this the earlier training can make some preparation. The candidate for the priesthood can be helped in advance to carry out his priestly functions in a seemly way, without ostentation and without hurry, remembering that the minds of others may work at a far slower pace than his own, especially when they are trying to follow unfamiliar paths. Too great a familiarity with the things of God may be the priest's most deadly temptation. He must also beware that his demeanour in the sanctuary does not become so 'stylized' as to suggest that he possesses some inhuman sanctity of his own. In approaching the God revealed by Jesus Christ all are sinners together.

The priest represents God to the people and the people to God. At the centre of his being there must be respect for those whom he represents; he is not their dictator but their friend and servant. Bishop Furse of St Albans once told students that an indispensable condition for the ministry is that 'you must like humans. A great many people like beetles and bugs and smells more than humans. Well, it takes all sorts to make a world. Don't take on this job of the ministry unless you really like humans. I remember someone coming to me and saying in a pious voice about a candidate for ordination that he thought he had a real love of souls. I said, "Oh, does he like humans? Is he really interested in human beings—women and children and odd things like that?" '[1] There is needed something of the quality of a Charles Lamb, who could shed tears of joy in the motley Strand at the spectacle of so much life; indeed of Jesus himself, who had compassion on the multitude because they were as sheep not having a shepherd.

The analogy of sheep and a shepherd is not one that would naturally occur in industrial cities nor even in suburbia; and its immediate translation into parochial terms is nowadays almost certainly a mistake; yet the candidate for the ministry is one who wants to share with others the good news which is transforming his own life; whose own life has been offered that it may be a perpetual invitation to 'taste and see how gracious the Lord is.' This will affect his attitudes to the rewards and securities towards which most men aspire; for he, more than most others, has wagered his life in the belief that less obvious rewards and less tangible securities are in the end more important. A worldly man of God is a contradiction; yet as the Son of God was implicated in the world he must be implicated too. 'The principle of Incarnation, as Christian theology understands it, is the principle of involvement. In Christ, we believe, God involved himself totally in our human predicament. How then, with regard to our own selves and psychic make-up, can we refuse to do the same?'[2] It is impossible in any lecture course or seminar to become fully aware of the depths

[1] *The World Task of the Christian Church* (SCM Press, 1925), p. 145.
[2] H. A. Williams in *Soundings: Essays Concerning Christian Understanding*, edited by A. R. Vidler (Cambridge, 1962), p. 73.

of human experience; but the student can be shewn that those depths exist. It is impossible also to explore its varieties; but the student will learn that the varieties are there and be prepared to meet them with understanding and respect. The understanding of human nature which has resulted from the researches of Sigmund Freud and his many followers and rivals is greatly to be welcomed; but no short course in psychology will provide a student with all he needs for his ministry. As in theology there are no ready-made answers so in psychology there can hardly be model diagnoses to provide a pattern for pastoral work. Yet much more needs to be done. There is much to be learned from the United States, where Clinical Pastoral Training has an important place in training for the ministry.

This is how it is set out in one University calendar:[1] 'Field work under approved supervision during at least one of the two summers preceding graduation is required for the degree of licentiate. The program of Clinical Pastoral Training is conducted by accredited chaplain supervisors in accredited institutions such as mental hospitals, general hospitals, penal and correctional centers, research centers and clinics. The program seeks to deepen the student's understanding of himself in his vocation through person to person relationships with troubled people to whom he seeks to minister. The program focuses on the experience of the student in the context of a pastoral situation under the dynamics of supervision in order to make it clear in understanding and practice the resources, methods and meanings of religion as expressed through pastoral care.' Those who have had this training are emphatic in their tributes to its value. Meanwhile the pioneer work of Dr Lake in this country, and the new centre he has set up at Nottingham, may provide something comparable, though for a much smaller proportion of ordinands.

The priest is to be the representative of people; through-

[1]The School of Theology of the University of the South, Sewanee, Tennessee, 1963.

out his ministry he will be learning to understand them better, not arranging them in types and classes but approaching each as an individual. This being respected as person is a fundamental need in life; and in modern life it is often denied. The Christian Church may well re-establish itself simply by caring in this way. It involves much listening and no judging; a readiness, on the face of it, to waste a lot of time. ('You have to waste a lot of time', said a bishop once to a group of clergy, 'but you can choose where you waste it.') If it is known that a priest is available, he is on his way to becoming effective.

There are horizons of service which can rarely be more than indicated during a time of training. (All the more need, it may be said, for clergy to have fresh opportunities of training when they have been at their work for some years.) In an approach to them the student may well learn that the achievements of psychology and the tradition and experience of the Church are not so alien to one another as he might have imagined. As has been said in another context, 'When, for example, the facts of human nature are being examined, a shrewd and experienced parish priest is entitled to compare what are said to be the scientifically established results with what he has himself learnt from his own trained insight and study. The literature of Christian saintliness must not be ignored.'[1]

The priest is called to be a steward of the mysteries of God. He may be said also to be a steward of the mysteries of man. There is for him no greater mystery and no greater wonder than that he should be placed between God and man, that his own life should be used sacramentally as 'instinct with God's redeeming purpose and man's response'; that through him the lost may be found, the despairing given purpose and hope, the sinful receive pardon.

[1]G. F. Woods in *Soundings*, p. 213.

6 · SPECIALISTS IN EVERYTHING?

In a provincial city the family of a well-known medical consultant had a very loyal maid-servant. When asked about her employer's particular sphere of practice she replied, 'Oh, he's a specialist in everything.'

That, indeed, is what parish priests are often expected to be—and odd-job men as well, who can use a typewriter and a duplicator, drive a car, operate a film projector and a tape recorder, cultivate a garden. ('No less than 395 out of 905 incumbents noted parsonage gardens as a time-consuming chore—very nearly every other clergyman', writes Mr Paul.[1]) Suggestions for the improvement of the priest's training inevitably propose new subjects for the curriculum. The situation is international. 'During the course of the last two or three generations', writes Dr Richard Niebuhr, 'the theological curriculum has been "enriched"—like vitamin impregnated bread—by the addition of a long series of short courses in sociology and social problems, rural and urban sociology, the theory of religious education, psychology of religion, psychology of counseling, methods of pastoral counseling, theory of missions, history of missions, methods of evangelism, theory and practice of worship, public speaking, church administration, et cetera, et cetera.'[2] Some of these courses might be differently named in England—and 'theory and practice of worship' is no outsider to be brought in as an extra—and there are probably fewer; but these additions are needed. Unless held in check they greatly increase in number. Every college regularly prepares itself to welcome the visiting specialist.

The staff of the Children's Council of the Church of England Board of Education conduct Teaching Weeks in twenty-two theological colleges. (Others accept similar help from Church Training Colleges for Teachers in the neighbour-

[1]*Deployment*, p. 131. [2]*Purpose*, p. 98.

hood.) Their purpose has been defined as (*a*) to give an introduction to the theory and practice of teaching by visiting local schools for practical teaching and observation; (*b*) to give some insight into the approach to children, in school and in the parish. Sometimes the course has been extended to include youth work and adult education; and the expert help of the appropriate Departments of the Board of Education has been called in. Visiting lecturers are usually supported by a group of tutors, chosen from clergy and children's work advisers who are available locally. These Teaching Weeks appear to be popular; the students show great interest and are grateful to those who give up their time to help them. The lecturers themselves, however, are wont to reflect upon the inadequacy of available time in which to transmit a basic skill which is invaluable for men whose future ministry will be engaged in teaching of many kinds.

The inside of a week is a short time; but other visiting specialists have less. All would probably be glad of more. They have to be content with the realization that there is a limit to the hours of a day and the weeks of a term.

The theological colleges do not only receive visiting specialists. Their students also make planned forays into the society in which their future ministry is to be exercised. They go to schools; they go to hospitals; they go to industry. Many a student from the south of England may find himself north of the Trent for the first time in his life, in a strange new world, whose appearance astonishes him, whose preoccupations are alien to anything he has known, and whose speech is not wholly comprehensible. (He may decide enthusiastically that he ought to have an experience of work in this part of the country, and be somewhat put aback to be told that a man who comes only for a short experience can do very little. He must be prepared to stay.) Other forays are organized as missions. A large group of students goes to a group of parishes, to help and to learn. They are not trippers. They have gone to work. Careful plans are made for these visits. The local clergy co-operate readily—not least in the hope that in the end one or two curates may be attracted to the deanery. The impression made in the area may not be lasting. A parishioner may recall the time when all those young men were around; and an incumbent may reflect that for a week or so he knew what it was like to have a staff available; but the impression made upon the visiting students may be much more lasting and profound. A fresh note of realism may be brought into many discussions; as it may also by those who have ventured, perhaps as far as Africa, in the scheme for Voluntary Service Overseas.

These projects have not mostly been planned long in advance. They represent a response to a changing situation and to immediate opportunities. There is hardly in the English theological colleges anything which can be compared to the periods of teaching practice which are so important for those who are in training as teachers. The possibilities of more carefully planned field work seem to need examination. Yet already by these different forms of visitation needs are being presented and personal aptitudes disclosed. A group of students who have been on mission together is different from what it was before the venture was undertaken.

It is not intended that clergy should be specialists in everything: 'Are all apostles? all prophets? all teachers?' asked Paul of the Corinthians (I Cor. 6.29-30). 'Do all work miracles? Have all gifts of healing? Do all speak in tongues of ecstasy? Can all interpret them?' The answer expected is 'No'.

Yet it may well be hoped that each priest should have some special interest, some chosen line of study, some expert knowledge and experience, even, which may lead others in the ministry to turn to him for help. Whether this be achieved or not it is important that all clergy should be aware of the different specialisms that exist and to know where expert help is available. None should be above calling in a consultant. Parochial life has too often witnessed the bungling of a personal problem by a well-meaning vicar who has been slow to call in expert help or has not known how to do so. In clerical meetings also the plaint is too often raised that what used to be the parson's job has been taken from him by the agencies of the welfare state; and the speaker has sometimes been ill-informed of the nature of those agencies and unwilling to recognize as partners those who are lifting from his shoulders the burden of much remedial work. A priest needs to recognize where help is needed and to know how it can be obtained. It may be from some fellow priest; it may be from some voluntary organization; it may be from some statutory agency.

This information can only be given very sketchily during preparatory study at a theological college. Post-Ordination Training[1]—in the setting of the diocese where the deacon or priest is working—is more important; and this is undertaken in most dioceses for a period of about three years after admission to the diaconate. The project faces many difficulties. There may be the geographical one of drawing together men from widely scattered parishes. There is the difficulty presented by the very different abilities and experience of the clergy who attend. The course may be repeating what has been done adequately in one college though hardly at all in another. But the chief difficulty is that of making this post-ordination training a first priority for the men concerned. A parish is delighted that, after a long delay, it has a curate once again; it is determined to use him to the full. The curate himself may be tempted to encourage this attitude. Surely he has left lecture rooms and tutorial groups behind at last? Why should he travel forty miles for a day's study when all around him sound the clamant demands of the work for which he has been trained? A vicar also may be sorry to let a man go—just when he might be taking a funeral or addressing a

[1]The reader is referred to ch. 6 of Basil Moss, *Clergy Training Today* and to Appendix 3 setting out the Post-Ordination Training in the Diocese of Bristol.

women's meeting or paying a round of visits. Many of these demands need to be resisted; most, indeed, can be circumvented. The director of post-ordination study needs to be given full authority from his Bishop to require the attendance of men at times which have been arranged well in advance. The Church needs apostles who are also disciples —messengers who are and never cease to be learners. It is not just a question of 'keeping up reading'; it is rather one of discerning a relationship between a living theology and a living discipleship.

In this period of post-ordination training the deacon or assistant priest should be encouraged to develop any aptitude which is already his; to make further exploration of fields of study which he has already entered; to test in practice conclusions which have come to him from reading or have been suggested to him by his teachers. He should be encouraged to go on examining the pre-suppositions on which his ministry is based and the traditions he has found accepted in the parish to which he has gone. He should be given further help with his preaching and speaking and teaching. In this period, also, he should be given what might be described as a map of the diocese in which he has been ordained, being shown where special work is being undertaken and where special resources are available. Industrial firms are often at pains to show newcomers to their factories the whole of the process in which normally they will perform only a very small part: it is equally important that the newcomer to the ordained ministry should be helped to realize with some imaginative understanding that the parish in which he serves represents only a small part of the Church engaged in mission throughout the area. Those who demonstrate the diocesan map can rarely, however, do so with any sense of satisfaction. There is so much work not being attempted because the workers are not available or because they are employed in the wrong way; because of a lack of vision, or because of inertia. This dissatisfaction is inevitably shared with these new recruits to the ordained ministry, and they are led again to consider priorities in the Christian mission. Tensions are inevitable; and can be creative.

At this point previous theological study gains in importance. The decision that from 1917 all candidates for the ministry should be graduates now belongs only to history. The latest information is that the number of graduates is under fifty per cent, though it is pointed out that the distinction between graduates and non-graduates is often unreal. 'Many of those without degrees are older candidates, some of whom have professional qualifications that are equivalent to a degree, and these men bring experience to their ministry from their years of lay work that will be of incalculable value.'[1] When this has been said, the proportion of graduates remains smaller than it should be; and the proportion of those who have read theology as a subject at the university remains, of course, much smaller still. It needs continually to be asked whether the Church is making the fullest use that it should of the Departments of Theology or of Biblical Studies in some of the newer Universities in the training of its candidates for the ministry. The university departments need students who follow these subjects with a practical aim in view. This might also help to divert them from too great an attention to minutiae or emphasis upon the inessential. The real purpose of theological study is not obscurity but clarity. A man who has deeply studied the basis of the Christian faith is less likely to be upset by criticism or turned aside by modes of thought which happen to be fashionable.

University study should have enabled him to relate these studies to others; and to respect the methods and conclusions of those who follow different paths. 'The student who discovers the way in which psychology or sociology or literary criticism can function as a mediating discipline between the gospel and contemporary man's search for faith has one of

[1]*Men for the Ministry* 1963, p. 9.

the prime requisites for a lifetime of fruitful reflection'[1]—and not of reflection only, but of action. From a consideration of such relationships his own thought may become fruitful and when to this is added a daily relationship with diverse men and women he will develop his own personal way of teaching and come to grips with the needs of men. If he has learned to relate the proclamation of the gospel to the findings of psychology he may be able also to co-operate with social workers; and to regard with a critical eye some proposals by public bodies which, for all their good intentions, are in danger of de-personalizing men and women. He is on the side of the social worker—often a lonely man or woman—even though he may be suspicious of social engineering.

This chapter has been a plea for the diversity of operations of which the apostle speaks[2]—a diversity of operations carried through by a diversity of people. From one point of view a priest's life is lonely; from another it is one that never ceases to be part of a corporate venture. He has many allies. Some are in the service of the Church—moral welfare workers, some teachers, secretaries of missionary societies, representatives of local Councils of Churches; others serve voluntary organizations or the State itself. They are in hospitals and libraries and schools and employment exchanges and police stations and public assistance offices. The probation officers are his allies; so are the health visitors and psychiatric social workers; and welfare officers in many industrial concerns. He should know these people, turn to them, and accept their help with gratitude. It has been a plea also for a recognition of diversities of operations among the clergy themselves—so that one naturally turns to another for the special help which he is qualified to give. It has further been a plea that each priest should be encouraged

[1]H. Richard Niebuhr, Daniel Day Williams and James F. Gustafson, *The Advancement of Theological Education* (New York: Harper & Bros., 1957), p. 102.

[2]I Cor. 12.4. The New English Bible has 'varieties of service'.

to follow his particular bent. He may have many talents or few: they are meant to be used; each is meant to make its contribution to the furtherance of that common mission upon which all are engaged.

An increasing number of men will probably be diverted from the parishes to other forms of ministry; as chaplains and lecturers in universities and training colleges; as chaplains in industry; as chaplains to the forces; as directors of religious education and chaplains for youth; as secretaries of the central organizations of the Church and of interdenominational enterprises; as teachers in schools—to say nothing of the long-term and short-term service which must be given within the Churches of Asia and Africa. These men need to be discovered early and to be given a special encouragement to follow their bent. Sometimes that encouragement is costly for the one who gives it. These are the very men who are most needed in the parishes! But they are also needed elsewhere; and must be encouraged to make the right preparation and to take the needed training. They may make other gifts to the parishes for which there will be gratitude—when, for example, the children of the parish grow up and go away from home to study; or sick parishioners are taken to a distant hospital—to find that a chaplain is there and at work. And in the end they may bring back into the service of the parishes an understanding of tasks to be attempted there and an ability to lead men and women to face them.

7 · RECRUITS FOR THE MINISTRY

English clergy returning on furlough to their own country from service in the Church overseas are often aghast at the numbers of clergy whom they encounter. When they find several priests occupied in leading the worship of a cathedral congregation which could best be described as sparse their comments are apt to be bitter. They may come from dioceses where a very few extra men might make a very great difference. On the other hand those who are responsible for organizing the assistance given by Readers in many dioceses in England know with how great difficulty the normal services in many parishes are maintained. Without the continual help of these laymen—operating often as a kind of flying squad sent out in different directions each week-end—much that is taken for granted might come to a standstill.

It is natural that harassed clergy frequently bemoan the fact that there are not sufficient recruits to join their number. In consequence gaps in the parochial ministry increase while opportunities there and in the non-parochial ministry cannot be used. The average age of the priesthood of the Church of England increases year by year, so that the derivation of the word priest from presbyter or elder is reinforced by observation. The office of the Council for the Ministry issues its graphs and tables to indicate how effective is the response each year to the call; parishes are alerted to be on the look-out for suitable men; and the whole Church is summoned to prayer that God's call may not go unanswered.

Nevertheless what is remarkable is not that there are so few newly-ordained clergy but that there are so many. Six hundred and thirty-five laymen were ordained in 1963 —that hardly gives the impression of a dying cause. They came from many previous occupations. There were many, of course, who made a steady progress, from school to university, from university to theological college, and so to kneel before the Bishop to be made deacons. Yet even for them the process has not been so straightforward as it might seem. They have not been in a pipe-line. They could not just decide to be ordained: however sure they might be in their own minds, their decision had to be approved by others. At one time National Service provided a testing interlude on the path to maturity. When it ceased to exist there have been bishops and examining chaplains who wished that they might have been able to invent it. Many of these young men have had vacation employment; some have spent a term in industry. They are genuine laymen. Yet, fairly soon after their twenty-third birthday, like so many before them, they were there in the cathedral, or in some parish church, not only being ordained by the Bishop, but taking an oath of allegiance to Her Majesty the Queen and declaring their assent to the Thirty-nine Articles of religion contained in the Book of Common Prayer.

Of the 635 new deacons in 1963, however, 124 were over forty years of age. These men have had many different occupations. Some have served in the forces, some have been civil servants, some schoolteachers; some have been employed in colonial administration, some in the professions, some in industry, some on the land, some in trade. In different ways each has heard the question 'Whom shall I send and who will go for us?' and made his personal response.

The real question before the Church is not how to secure more men but how to use the men it already has. Bishop Selwyn's '"*sacramentum*" of obedience. "Here am I, send me"; "I go, Sir", as well understood as in the army and navy' may be operative in some Provinces of the Anglican Communion but it is not a characteristic mark of the Church of England. The life of the Church is not yet directed to this end. Yet another aim enunciated by Bishop Selwyn—even before he went to New Zealand—has been partially attained. He was writing from Eton in May 1837, that ordination candidates should be derived 'from that class from which Christ selected his apostles—from the poor. Let the Church take root downwards. Let every peasant in the country have an interest in the Establishment in the person of a son, or brother, or cousin. We have the best materials for the formation of a plebeian ministry that ever were possessed by any nation.'[1] This may be a somewhat romanticized description of the fishermen disciples—who must have

[1]H. W. Tucker, *op. cit.* I, p. 44.

been capitalists in a small way—but it represented a nineteenth-century and still represents a twentieth-century need. In New Zealand Selwyn found no room for what he called the 'gentleman heresy'. Yet this heresy long affected the Church of England. A gentleman in every parish was the ideal. Since the end of the eighteenth century there were some small funds available to help those who otherwise could not afford the university course; and the first theological colleges were in the Isle of Man and Cumberland and Cardiganshire, to train men for areas into which graduates of Oxford and Cambridge did not penetrate in great numbers.[1] But the 'plebeian' candidates were often lost by the 'Establishment' to the ministries of other Churches. The 1914-1918 war, however, evoked a multitude of ordination candidates from all ranks in the forces and from great varieties of social background; and when chaplains assembled the first tide of these at the old Machine Gun School at Le Touquet, they were visited by Randall Davidson, Archbishop of Canterbury, who repeated an earlier pledge that means would be found by which these volunteers—if suitable—would be trained for the ministry.[2] Suitability had, of course, to be tested; and the improvised school at Le Touquet became the Ordination Test School in the disused gaol at Knutsford under the leadership of the Rev. F. R. Barry. There were many difficulties yet to be faced, but the pledge was honoured; gradually the training of men for the ministry became a heavy charge upon the central funds of the Church of England.

In the days of the 'gentleman heresy', of course, things were different. 'Abstract the clergy from the rural parishes,' asked Mark Pattison in 1868, 'and how much cultivation would you have left? Literary men who lead a metropolitan life are apt to think deprecatingly of the clergy as a class. They would do well to consider the immense advantage

[1]Chadwick, *op. cit.*, p. 3.
[2]R. V. H. Burne, *Knutsford. The Story of the Ordination Test School* 1918-41 (SPCK, 1960), p. 2.

which England enjoys, in comparison with a Catholic country, by the possession of a territorially endowed clergy, and the circumstance that the clergy receive a general, not a professional education.'[1] From the point of view of the ordaining bishop it was usually sufficient that the candidate was a graduate of Oxford or Cambridge. It needs to be remembered that these universities were Anglican institutions with credal tests. Degrees were restricted to those who accepted membership of the Church. There was compulsory chapel attendance. The heads of colleges were mostly clergy, as were many of the fellows. 'Even in 1840 something like half of the population of the two universities expected to take orders. The purpose of the university bore an imperfect but recognizable resemblance to the purpose of a modern theological college; to have demanded a further period of collegiate life seemed redundant and absurd.'[2]

Reasons for the foundation of theological colleges were many. The universities were changing. They could no longer be regarded as Anglican preserves. Nor could they supply a sufficient number of men for the new parishes of an industrialized England. Moreover there was a realization that training had not been good enough. Something more professional was needed; something in which the devotional life of prayer and meditation played a greater part. This expressed itself partly through the foundation of what came to be known as party colleges, where the teaching was either soundly Tractarian or definitely Evangelical. Yet dissatisfaction was more widely felt than this. It is significant that when in 1856 a suggestion was made to the Wesleyan Methodists that they should return to the Church of England, the first of four obstacles listed by them was 'the impression that the Church of England was not sufficiently careful concerning her selection of clergy'.[3] It was being

[1]*Suggestions on Academical Organization* (Edinburgh: Edmonston and Douglas, 1868), p. 35. [2]Chadwick, *op. cit.*, p. 2.

[3]Edward Carpenter in *From Uniformity to Unity*, ed. Nuttall and Chadwick (SPCK, 1962), p. 331.

realized at last that the ministry of the Church could not be left to take care of itself. From New Zealand Bishop Selwyn criticized the foundation of St Augustine's College in the English Canterbury because it was likely to create a division between the well trained working clergy and those who were content to be clerical gentlemen. It is significant that when a principal was sought for the theological college founded at Wells in 1840 those responsible chose J. H. Pinder who from 1829 to 1835 had been Principal of Codrington College, Barbados, where he had prepared twenty-seven candidates for ordination. The curriculum at Wells was closely modelled upon that at Codrington.

Theological colleges were developing in two ways. Some provided an alternative to university training—partly for those who could not afford it, partly for those who were not gifted academically, partly for older men who did not want to waste time and were keen to be at work as soon as possible. Others provided an optional extra to university education, with an emphasis upon pastoral and devotional preparation; while some colleges accepted students from both sources. For those who had come from a university the theological college was something in the nature of a retreat. S. C. Carpenter refers to the 'secluded atmosphere of the Theological College, with its happy family life and its strictly ordered day' where 'men learn two lessons of lifelong value, that Christians are brothers and that prayer is a reality. A man may arrive at his Theological College in the middle of a term and he will have what seems to him the remarkable experience of being accepted as a friend at once, without any necessity for the slow breaking of preliminary ice. And he will learn, not so much from the Principal, Vice-Principal, or Chaplain—that he perhaps takes for granted, but from his fellow-students—that it is possible for a raw young man, fresh from the rather casual life of the University, to worship with others three or four times every day, and to spend half an hour every day in the practice of private meditation. He does not always maintain throughout his ordained life all the habits that he learned at Cuddesdon or Wells, but even if his first eager freshness be dimmed by the spirit of the world, or his prayer-time diminished by the incessant necessity of what is known as work, he has for a year or longer had a devout and unworldly standard set before him.'[1]

The quotation indicates the strength of the theological college as it has been inherited in this century: it may also suggest some of its weaknesses. Dean Carpenter was recalling a small college with a small staff. The family atmosphere of such a college has usually been commended by former students—but might it not sometimes be a little precious? Nowadays the frontiers of the working world penetrate even into the most Trollopean surroundings of cathedral cities; students are often disturbed rather than immediately encouraged by what they hear and the discussions in which they take part. This combines with the adjustment that they must make to the calling upon which they are entering and an inevitable tension is set up. The Rev. T. Ralph Morton, writing from an experience over the past twenty-five years of meeting in the Iona Community young men from the theological colleges of many denominations who have completed their training and are at the outset of their ministry has recorded some disturbing conclusions. 'Certain impressions', he writes, 'grow with the years.

'The first is that these men were much freer in their relations with other men and much more able to communicate with them before they entered a theological college than afterwards.

'The second impression is that, despite the greater attention given in theological colleges to professional training, the gap between the studies of the colleges and the work of the Church to which the students go is too wide for them to jump. . . .

'The third impression is of the very strong but quite

[1]*Church and People*, 1789-1889 (SPCK, 1933), p. 272.

distinct way of thinking that each college imposes on its students. The colleges seem to want to produce conformists and not experimenters.

'The fourth and final impression is of the depressing effect of theological education on those who endure it. Many come out of the theological colleges disillusioned and in despair. Those who have not become disillusioned have, all too often, given up all intention of seeking for new ways and a deeper obedience in the life of the Church.'[1]

This is searching criticism; and no doubt there is an answer to some of it. But the fact that it can be made is an indication that the motto 'as it was in the beginning is now and ever shall be' will not do for theological education. The Church of England, indeed, is constantly examining the situation afresh. But at the moment it is still true that none of the Colleges belongs to the Church as a whole. All bear the marks of their history, having originated as local or private —and sometimes private party—ventures. A small staff—the principal, vice-principal and chaplain to whom Dean Carpenter referred were long considered sufficient—may be adequate for pastoral and devotional preparation; but for the preparation of those who will think theologically and relate their thinking to the life of men and women in the social conditions of the present day a larger staff is certainly needed. Seclusion also may be all very well; but those who are being trained will have little seclusion in the future and they will work among people who have less. Colleges in Manchester and in Leeds might be in the right place for some students; but colleges in Manchester and in Leeds are the ones that have died. If the Church is to develop colleges of its own in the future certain criteria need to be taken into account. A college should be related to a University—preferably one of the newer ones which the Church has neglected so much in the past. It should be related to an urban setting. It should be linked with other training

[1]Mark Gibbs and T. Ralph Morton, *God's Frozen People* (Collins, Fontana Books, 1964), p. 160.

institutions; with a teacher-training college, for example, and with a Department of Social Studies. There should be coming and going between students in these different educational disciplines; coming and going also between the students of different denominations. It may be that Queen's College in Birmingham is destined to be the pioneer on these lines.[1]

The nineteenth century suggested another way of training for the ministry as well as the theological college. In the east end of Doncaster Parish Church there is an inscription stating that the reredos was built as 'the grateful and loving gift of eighty-eight of those graduates of Oxford and Cambridge who here prepared themselves for Holy Orders under the instruction and guidance of the Rev. C. J. Vaughan, D.D., Vicar of Doncaster.' (The verb is significant: they 'prepared themselves' not 'were prepared'.) Vaughan had been a great Headmaster of Harrow from 1844 to 1859. In Doncaster he found himself in a situation for which most of the clergy of the Church were not ready. His dissatisfaction expressed itself in a University Sermon preached at Cambridge on Trinity Sunday, 1861.[2] He did not want to see training for the ministry separated from the universities. 'The freer intercourse which a University offers of mind with mind, the larger choice and mutual correction or instructors, not to mention the ampler gifts of learning and ability which such a place affords in its teachers, are invaluable aids in the study of a true theology.' The validity of the argument remains. But he did not want these men from the universities to be thrown into the parishes to sink or swim, to make fools of themselves unnecessarily. 'Does it come naturally to any man, when once he is a master of scriptural doctrine, to manage a parochial school, to organize

[1]The reader is referred to chapter 5 in *Clergy Training Today* by Basil S. Moss.

[2]The sermon is set out in full in *The Word of Life*, edited by R. R. Williams (SPCK, 1960), pp. 6ff.

parochial visiting, to catechize the young, to visit the sick, or to prepare and preach sermons? It may be so with some few men.... But surely this is not a common, certainly it is not the normal condition of a candidate for Holy Orders. Certainly it is not the course pursued by a student of law, or tolerated in a student of medicine.' So he went on to invite those of his hearers who might wish to do so to join him in his parish and learn the tasks of a parish priest experimentally. Vaughan went from Doncaster to be Master of the Temple and later Dean of Llandaff, where he died in 1897, but all the time he was training men for the ministry, more than four hundred of them in all, including a future Archbishop of Canterbury, Randall Davidson.

Vaughan's work was personal. He created no continuing institution nor would he have wished to do so. From time to time others have experimented on the same lines; but there has been no large scale enterprise by the Church as a whole. The Church has rather accepted the existing theological colleges, some created by dioceses and others by private enterprise, aiding them and supplementing them as seems fit. A development which was once suspect—'hothouse' was the adjective applied by critics to the atmosphere of the colleges—has been accepted as normal and necessary. In 1909 the Upper House of the Convocation of Canterbury resolved that after January 1917 'candidates for holy orders be required (in addition to a university degree) to have received at least one year's practical and devotional training at a recognized theological college, or under some other authorized supervision'. This insistence upon a university degree, which disturbed the Protestants at Highbury and infuriated the Catholics at Kelham, was defeated by the urgencies of the situation; but there are few men ordained in the Church of England today who have not spent some time at a theological college.

Amongst the agencies recognized by the Church of England as Theological Colleges—just short of thirty of them—are Rochester, founded in 1959 to cater for the 30-40 age group, Worcester, founded in 1952 for men over forty, and the non-residential Southwark Ordination Course, founded in 1960. This works through evening classes and a series of residential week-ends. It exists 'to train men for Holy Orders from as wide a variety of background and experience as possible and with no limitation of age. It is open both to men who wish to serve a full-time parochial ministry and to men who wish to engage in some form of supplementary ministry.' The first men were ordained from this course at Michaelmas 1963.

Before men are accepted for training for the ministry of the Church of England they must be approved, not merely by the bishop who is to ordain them, but—and this is new since the War—by a specially chosen team at a Selection Conference organized by the Council for the Ministry. Twenty candidates attend each of these and five selectors. They are held from a Monday to a Thursday and they are held in almost every week of the year. Of the selectors it has been written: 'Each is nominated by his bishop, and the bishops regularly revise their lists. Each serves at most once a year and usually less often than that. They are often unknown to their colleagues when they arrive at the conference but very quickly indeed they form a team. Each team is different: the same five selectors will never serve together again. The lay selector, a most important and valuable member of the team, may be a schoolmaster or university don, an industrialist or professional man, a farmer or a retired officer of one of the services. All are chosen by their bishops as faithful churchmen who are experienced in the assessment of men. Every candidate will have a private interview during the conference with each selector.'[1]

It is not until the candidates have left that decisions are made, whether the candidate be recommended to go forward to training, whether he be deferred, or whether he be told that in the opinion of the selectors his best service to the

[1] *Men for the Ministry* 1963, p. 6.

Church will be to continue as a layman. Mistakes, of course, can be made; but there is a wonderful unanimity of decision; and if a bishop feels that any candidate should be reconsidered he may ask for him to attend another selection conference. The word 'conference' is a fitting one to describe what takes place. Selectors and candidates confer together. There is a fresh setting forth of the task of the Church in the present age, the resources for that task, and the need not only for those who will be ordained but for the committed layman, taking his part—and by no means a second best—in the ministry of the people of God. The purpose of what is done is to discover what the Holy Spirit is saying to each of the men present, to what form of service he is calling him. Those of us who were ordained in earlier days may sometimes wonder whether we should ever have been passed by the selectors; but this new system has been called one of the best things that has happened to the Church of England since the war. It represents, at an early stage, the concern of the Christian community, the larger Church, which should always have a share in the selection and approval of those who are to be ordained. It makes a return to the old, haphazard days well nigh unthinkable.

8 · SOME QUESTIONS THAT REMAIN

At the conclusion of most detective stories there is a chapter in which loose ends are tied up and the reader's remaining questions are answered. No such reward awaits the reader of this contribution. There is no neat solution. The questions remain. We are concerned with the pilgrim people of God and different tasks to be carried through by those who exercise a ministry among them. There are tasks that remain permanent; there are tasks that change; and there are some to be attempted which seem quite new, occasioned by the nature of the terrain through which the pilgrims move and by the people they encounter on the way. But there is no end to journeying. We are strangers and sojourners as all our fathers were.

Nevertheless some of the questions which remain can be isolated for consideration. Is it right that there should be a campaign to secure recruits for the ordained ministry? Does not God choose his own? The Council for the Ministry, we read, 'has now for the first time a full-time Recruitment Secretary. It will be his task to stimulate and co-ordinate much of the good work that is already being done in this field by means of fellowships of vocation, school visits, enquirers' conferences and in many other ways; and to try to find out in consultation with others what the forces are which lead some young men to offer themselves for ordination and what are the forces which deter others whom God may be calling.'[1] Within these limits the appointment seems wise; for there are still those who, for no good reasons, decide that the calling is not for them, that it is quite out of the question. A widespread dissemination of information is still needed.

God's call has always reached men and women in great varieties of ways. He does not compel. He offers a choice. The late Sir George Adam Smith reflected upon this in his great exposition of the Book of Isaiah and the call of the prophet described in chapter six. 'What is a call to the ministry of God? . . . Isaiah got no "call" in our conventional sense of the word, no compulsion that he must go, no articulate voice describing him as the sort of man needed for the work. . . . After passing through the fundamental religious experience of forgiveness and cleansing, which are in every case the indispensable premises of life with God, Isaiah was left to himself. No direct summons was addressed to him, no compulsion was laid on him; but he heard the voice of God asking generally for messengers, and he was immediately full of the mind that he was the man for the mission, and of the heart to give himself to it. So great an example cannot be too closely studied by candidates for

[1] *Men for the Ministry* 1964, p. 5.

the ministry in our own day. Sacrifice is not the half-sleepy, half-reluctant submission to the force of circumstance or opinion, in which shape it is so often travestied among us, but the resolute self-surrender and willing resignation of a free and reasonable soul. . . . *We*—not God—have to make the decision. We are not to be dead, but living, sacrifices, and everything which renders us less than fully alive both mars at the time the sincerity of our surrender and reacts for evil upon the whole of our subsequent ministry.'[1] There was a time when it might be said that some men had drifted into the ministry. That would hardly be said today. Too many decisions have to be made. But the call, 'Whom shall I send and who will go for us?' is still heard in the world and may still evoke the old response.

God calls both men and women; and if the thesis of the ministry as that of the whole people of God be accepted, the ministry of women must be a very great one. Indeed it has been a great one from the first. Yet this has been only grudgingly accepted by the largely male leadership of the Church; the opportunities for leadership accorded to women have mostly been few; and those who have entered full-time service of the Church have mostly been poorly paid. The question of the place of women within the ordained ministry is one which different Churches have answered differently: within Anglicanism it will long remain a matter of discussion and debate. This book has not ventured upon these issues, but it must be emphasized that the place of women within the ministry of the Church—within its diverse ministries—is one of the great questions that remain.

The Recruitment Secretary, appointed by the Council for the Ministry, is charged to endeavour to discover what are the forces which deter from offering themselves for training some whom God may be calling. One factor may be that of subscription to the Thirty-nine Articles. This is, of course, an old story. In 1863 A. P. Stanley, Dean of Westminster,

[1] *The Book of Isaiah* (Hodder and Stoughton, 1927), Vol. I, pp. 75 f.

published a *Letter to the Lord Bishop of London on the State of Subscription in the Church of England and in the University of Oxford.* He wrote of 'the greatest of all calamities to the Church of England in the gradual falling off in the supply of the intelligent, thoughtful and highly-educated young men who, twenty and thirty years ago were to be found at every ordination'.[1] Has the same thing happened a hundred years later? Stanley's initiative, it is to be remembered, was effective. A royal commission was appointed, and the present form of subscription was proposed and—though dissentient voices were raised—agreed upon by the Convocations.

> I assent to the Thirty-nine Articles of Religion and to the Book of Common Prayer, and of Ordering of Bishops, Priests, and Deacons; I believe the doctrine of the Church of England as therein set forth to be agreeable to the Word of God; and in public prayer and administration of the Sacraments I will use the form in the said book prescribed and none other, except so far as shall be ordered by lawful authority.

The meaning of the phrase 'lawful authority' is still a matter of clerical debate; but the most widely-used manual on the Thirty-nine Articles points out that 'the change of language in the form of subscription was deliberate. We are asked to affirm today, not that the Articles are all agreeable to the Word of God, but that the doctrine of the Church of England as set forth in the Articles is agreeable to the Word of God. That is, we are not called to assent to every phrase or detail of the Articles but only to their general sense. This alteration was made of set purpose to afford relief to scrupulous consciences.'[2] Be that as it may, the position remains unsatisfactory and open to great misunderstanding. It is probably right that much of the doctrinal teaching in

[1]T. E. Prothero, *Life and Letters of Dean Stanley* (Thomas Nelson & Sons, cheap pocket edition, 1909), p. 339.

[2]E. J. Bicknell, *The Thirty-nine Articles*, third edition, revised by H. J. Carpenter (Longmans, 1955), p. 21.

theological colleges is in the form of a commentary on the Articles; for they represent what Hensley Henson once called the 'platform' of the Church of England. Yet the present Dean of St Paul's is only one of those who desire revision of these doctrinal statements. 'After all', he writes, 'it would be a miracle if a summary of Christian doctrine drawn up in the sixteenth century had proved to be adequate in the twentieth, after the transformation of our civilization and our culture by the rise and progress of natural science and historical criticism. That miracle has not happened. My plea is that the time is long overdue to admit that fact and to take the appropriate action.'[1] Students in the theological colleges no doubt occasionally express themselves rather less temperately on this subject. But the Dean's words are forcible enough: 'I look forward to a time when a candidate for ordination will no longer be confronted with a series of theological propositions to which any well-informed man can assent only with reservation and reserves, but with a statement of the gospel which he is to preach, which he can sign with uplifted heart and a clear mind.'[2] The possible union of the Church of England with the Methodist Church raises the question of Establishment in a new way; and it needs to be remembered that the form of subscription to the Articles now used was one agreed upon by Parliament though accepted by the Convocations. What kind of subscription will be expected from a candidate for the ministry in a re-united Church? This is one of the questions that remain.

One of the factors deterring men from offering themselves for training for the ministry is that they are married, some of them having young families. In earlier days the curate was often unmarried: the very fact that he was free from family obligations made it more likely that he could accept

[1]W. R. Matthews, *The Thirty-nine Articles. A Plea for a New Statement of the Christian Faith as understood by the Church of England* (Hodder and Stoughton, 1961), p. 24.
[2]*Ibid.*, p. 34.

work in an industrial parish in the North or a slum parish in the East End of London. The situation has greatly changed. Thirty years ago married undergraduates were very rare indeed; but at the beginning of the Michaelmas term at Oxford in 1963 the problem was being faced that there were four hundred married undergraduates for whom no suitable accommodation was available. In some theological colleges a third of the students are married. Attempts are made to provide houses or flats for these; but the difficulty is often great; as may be the financial difficulties faced by the married couples also. Many wives go out to work; but not all can do this. Should the central funds of the Church be used to support the wives and families of men who have been accepted for training? This has not been done up to the present, though the Train a Priest Fund raised by the *Church Times* each Lent provides help which is invaluable, and older ordination funds can be diverted for this purpose also. This question remains. The theological colleges are also giving thought to the help which they can give to the wives of candidates for the ministry, to help them in a ministry which they must inevitably share—if it be only as one who answers a vicarage door.

It has already been emphasized that there are varieties of ministry, some to be exercised by lay people and some by ordained clergy. Within the ranks of those who prepare to be ordained ought there to be an attempted unity of preparation or should attempts be made to discern and develop different aptitudes? In the courses taken by intended teachers at Training Colleges some specialize, for example, in rural science and others in physical education. Should there be special preparation for the man who intends to be a country parson? When men are needed for particular types of ministry—for example, to be a chaplain at a College of Advanced Technology—the question at once is raised, where are such men to be found, and who is to assess their aptitude for what may be a pioneer and experimental post? Already there is an inevitable distinction between graduate and non-graduate candidates—though we are constantly being reminded that all the ability is not among the graduates. Yet there are those who can take the General Ordination Examination in their stride while there are others for whom it is a high hurdle. Any suggestion of a staff college is resisted, not least by college principals who do not wish to see their potentially most promising students—students with a particular contribution to make to their fellows and to the community life—prematurely 'creamed off'. Failing this, there is need for a multiplicity of forms of 'in-service' training. One of their advantages might well be that clergy would receive special training alongside other men and women. Thus there may develop a partnership of concern with doctors, social workers, schoolteachers, marriage guidance counsellors, and with the growing number of people more or less intimately concerned with the personal relationships of men and women. The clergy needed in the parishes are men who know what goes on in a hospital and in a juvenile court, at an inquest and in a municipal committee, at trade-union meetings and in the office of the local newspaper.

There has been much discussion in recent years of 'part-time priests' and 'supplementary ministries'; and it is to be recalled that the Southwark Ordination Course is open both for those who wish to serve a full-time parochial ministry and to those who wish to engage in some form of supplementary ministry. It is tempting to regard these suggestions as being designed to meet pressing needs by the calling up of a second reserve of volunteers. The new proposals however are derived partly from a fresh consideration of the ministry of the whole Church as it is to be discerned in the pages of the New Testament and partly from a quickened understanding of the nature and task of the Church as it is seen in a missionary situation. As the report of a discussion of these suggestions prepared for the World Council of Churches has put it, 'In a static society, or in a situation where the congregation no longer regards itself as a missionary community, this institutionalizing of the ministry will not create any immediately apparent difficulties. There will be plenty of time to recruit and train new ministers from each generation to replace those who die. But when the Church is in the midst of a dynamic society, where it is challenged to move constantly into new situations or into new areas with the ministry of reconciliation, this restriction of the ministry to a highly institutionalized professional class will make it impossible for the Church to move swiftly and effectively. What is needed in such a situation is a variety of forms of ministry appropriate to the new situation in which the Church has to make its apostolic witness.'[1] Anglican history provides many commentaries on these dangers. Nor are they yet entirely overcome.

Within the Anglican Communion the most notable experiment in providing a supplementary ministry has taken place in the Diocese of Hong Kong. Thirteen men have been ordained under a special canon of the Chinese Church regulating the ordination of men who would remain in their secular employments. It is interesting to learn that this has not meant the dilution of a graduate ministry by the introduction of non-graduates but rather the reverse. 'Of these thirteen men, eight are schoolmasters with university degrees, and of the other five two are university graduates. When this auxiliary ministry was introduced none of the regular local clergy were graduates. Now all the younger full-time clergy are graduates, and the number of the full-time ministry has grown from four twenty years ago to seventeen today.'[2]

This book is largely concerned with training for the ministry. An equally important question is the restoration of the ministry, ten, twenty, thirty years after men have been ordained. A time of retreat is, of course, what is usually prescribed; and no doubt it is often the right prescription.

[1] *A Tent-Making Ministry. Towards a More Flexible Form of Ministry* (World Council of Churches, 1963), p. 5.
[2] *Ibid.*, p. 12.

Under wise guidance the spiritual life becomes real once more and, through the mercy of God, spiritual vitality is restored. But there is a need also for restoration of intellectual activity. Why has the Vicar never anything new to say? What is wrong with his sermons? It may perhaps be because his mind is no longer put to the stretch by the demands of exacting reading. He has got into the habit of making do with book reviews. And that will not suffice. There is needed a depth in intellectual life as well as in spiritual life. Little help is to be gained from shallow men. But reading is not enough. What those who do much talking often most need is to listen; to hear a new voice bringing fresh illumination to familiar questions; to be stimulated by the clash of mind upon mind. This is well known to the bishops and directors of religious education; but they often conclude that those who most need the help which the clergy schools they provide may give are those who are least likely to attend.

There is needed width also. Why is it that so many clergy know so little, for example, about the World Council of Churches, and only awake to the claims and significance of the Anglican Communion every ten years when publicity is given to the assembling of a Lambeth Conference? No doubt they are too busy to keep in touch with movements which seem far off. But can insularity be excused? A knowledge of what is happening elsewhere may bring fresh inspiration to their ministry and fresh encouragement to their people, as well as leading both to examine more critically parochial claims which seemed so important and parochial expenditure which seemed so praiseworthy. It might also prevent the 'we' and 'they' division which is an obstacle to the effective work of the Church in our day. There are 'they' who attend diocesan committees, and boards in Westminster, who travel to conferences abroad while 'we' get on with the front-line work in the parishes. Or it may be 'we' who have seen some new vision of what the Church might be doing and wonder how we are ever going to be able to get it across to the traditionalists in the parishes. Many illustrations of this theme might be made. These divisions do great harm. All are in need of restoration, both spiritual and intellectual; and one of the tasks of the future is to discover how this may be secured in times which are always busy.

This is an age of great problems but of much superficial triviality. The minister must continually be concerned with little things. His temptation is also to be trivial. He will be redeemed from this, as his ministry proceeds, if he is constantly storing up growing reserves upon which he can draw. Happy is the man who has begun to do this early. The importance of training for the ministry is that the minister learns to be in training always. He can hardly speak the apostolic word unless he is always a disciple, that is, a learner. For him the questions and the tasks remain. And they remain great.

II

The Church of Scotland

JAMES WHYTE

1 · A TRADITION UNDER FIRE

THERE is an interesting passage in *The Book of Discipline*, 1560, which tells us much about the traditional Scottish attitude to the ministry. In this basic document of the Scottish Reformation a high standard is set for the 'Election, Examination and Admission of Ministers', and the authors go on: 'We are not ignorant, that the raritie of godlie and learned men sall seme to some a just reassone quhy that so strait and scharpe examinatioun suld not be takin universallie; for so it sall appeir, that the most parte of Kirkis sall haif no Minister at all: But let these men understand, that the lack of able men sall nott excuse us befoir God, gif by oure consent unable men be placed over the floke of Christ Jesus; ...' They suggest that it is better to have no minister at all than to be satisfied with 'a vane schaddow', and end, 'For we can nott juge him a dispensatour of Goddis mysteries, that in no wyise can breke the breid of lyif to the faynting and hungrie saulis; neather juge we that the Sacramentis can be rychtlie ministred by him, in quhais mouth God hes put no sermon of exhortatioun.'

Here we have a peep into a controversy about whether, in a time of shortage of ministers, standards of entry should be made low. The fact that in a time of severe shortage they were fixed high, and that it was thought better to have no ministers at all than poorly qualified ones, indicates the view of the ministry which became the tradition of the Church of Scotland. The ministry is thought of in terms of function, as a job to be done, rather than in terms of privilege or status; it is thought of, therefore, in terms of ability rather than of validity. Since the key function of the ministry was the preaching and teaching of the Word, the faithful exposition of Scripture in public and in private, there was required not only the inner call of the Spirit, but also the outer call of the Church, which made 'scharpe examinatioun' of the candidate's ability. The Scottish reformers believed that the Ministry of Word and Sacrament was a gift of Christ to his Church and that through it Christ himself spoke to, and ruled, his people, using the ministry of men as his instrument. Nevertheless, they did not expect that the ability to exercise this ministry would normally be given apart from the processes of learning and study, and so they required an educated ministry, able to read the Scriptures in the original Hebrew and Greek, and learned in the history and theology of the Church.

Their ideal was not simply an educated ministry, but an educated people, and plans were put forward for primary, secondary and University education. Not all, alas, were put into effect, and some not for centuries, for other men had baser uses for the funds which might have been devoted to the education of Scotland. Yet a high standard of general education was attained, and the fact that at one time Scotland had five Universities when England had two is worthy of note. The broad-based general M.A. degree of the Scottish universities was the propaedeutic for professional specialization in Law, Medicine and Divinity.

The Divinity Faculty of the University educated men for the Church's ministry. Not till the nineteenth century was a degree of B.D. instituted, and it has never been required by the Church that its students take the degree. When, through Secessions and finally the Disruption, other Presbyterian Churches came into being in Scotland, they founded Divinity Colleges, in which the curriculum followed the same pattern as that in the Divinity Faculties, with one or two interesting additions, the most lasting of which has been Practical Theology. At the Union of the two great Presbyterian Churches in Scotland in 1929 Colleges and Faculties were also united, and the curriculum laid down (to be undertaken after an Arts degree or a course equivalent to it) was a three-year course of study with five departments —Old Testament, New Testament, Church History, Systematic Theology and Practical Theology. This is still substantially the shape of the course advocated by Andrew Melville in 1589.

Since 1929, and particularly since the Second World War, the course has been under repeated attack, and under repeated review. The demands for more practical training, for more time to be given to courses in Pastoral Counselling, Teaching Methods, Sociology, Industry, for more attention to the devotional life, and for more corporate spiritual discipline, for less time (or no time at all) to be devoted to Hebrew and Greek—all these have been met, modified, or rejected from time to time, but no basic changes have been made. When the Church modified its requirements for men over 25 (later, 23) it was in order that those who received a call later in life, lacking the full qualifications for University entrance, might still have an opportunity to enter the ministry. Many men of outstanding ability have entered the ministry in this way. The modified curriculum was never intended to produce a second-class minister, inferior in any way to his fellows. In fact, the five-year course includes the full theological curriculum, and it is only recently that such students have been excused the study of Hebrew. Yet it has been said, and not without justification, that the course had become easy to enter and almost impossible to fail. An objective standard is now set by requiring all students to complete at least the Licentiate in Theology of the Scottish Universities. Students in the regular course must still do Hebrew as well as Greek. In two of the four University centres, Practical Theology is a University Department, and is now examined for the B.D. degree; in the other two it is a church subject, taught apart from the University.

'Field work' is now supervised by Boards of Practical Training, to ensure that what the student does contributes to his preparation for the ministry, but even more, that it does not interfere with his academic work! A supervised probationary year is normally required, which is usually spent in a full-time assistantship. During this year the probationer will in future attend two residential courses, in which some of the subjects which have not found a place in the crowded curriculum, and some which can be better studied after some experience of pastoral work, will be dealt with in an intensive way.

All these things, however, represent modifications and additions to a course whose basic pattern is unchanged since 1589. This is, of course, a deceptively misleading statement, since if one examined the content of the instruction given in the departments of study, the differences would immediately be apparent. Form Criticism and the theology of Paul Tillich are far enough removed from Calvinist scholasticism. Students today are more likely to be ignorant of the Westminster Confession of Faith than of the theology of Bultmann. Yet the course remains primarily an academic course, and while it produces each year its crop of competent B.D.'s, it allows through into the ministry a considerable number of men who neither attain, nor indeed aspire to, any academic competence. These are of two kinds. There is a not insignificant minority of men who cause despair to their teachers by their ability to pass examinations without exposing their minds to any new influences at all. Some, of course, wrestle valiantly and painfully with teaching that contradicts their fundamentalist beliefs; theirs is a hard but honest road. But there is a disturbing number of tight-shut minds, who treat everything in the course as a task to be done, like a crossword puzzle, without any relevance to their faith or their future ministry. Little can be done for these, save to hope that the Church will cease to accept them in the first place. The other kind of non-academic, however, presents a much more important challenge to the course, for he is the kind of person most people (including, often, his teachers) feel will make a good minister. He is kind and warm-hearted, and really interested in people—much more interested in people than in ideas. His congregation, one feels, will confide in him, and not be disappointed. His Kirk Session will soon become a happy and friendly body. His enthusiasms will be catching, not offensive. His Hebrew Bible will be closed for the last time after his final examinations, and it is doubtful how often his Greek Testament will be used. His thin knowledge of Divinity will be supplemented, one fears, by no more than a few popular books in the years to come: he will have neither time nor inclination for anything heavier. His sermons will not be very profound, but they will not be very long either. Some congregation will love him, and thank God for him. The challenge which such a man brings to the course is this: the gifts which he brings to the ministry do not seem to be those which the course is designed to nourish and increase; he has survived the course, but it can hardly be said that he has benefited by it. At least three different conclusions might be drawn from this. Either the course is totally or largely irrelevant to the needs of the ministry today, or the idea that such men make good ministers (as distinct from well-liked ones) is based on a mistaken idea of what the ministry is for, or we ought to prepare two kinds of minister, the one academic, the B.D., the theologian, for whom the present course seems designed, and the other non-academic, the practical, the unintellectual, for whom a course of a quite different kind would be required.

The third possibility is not likely to be seriously considered in Scotland, for however near we come to it in practice we have never in theory accepted the idea of two kinds or grades of minister; perhaps Presbyterianism itself makes this difficult. Talent may vary greatly from individual to individual, but the Church makes the same basic demands of those whom it ordains to the Ministry of Word and Sacrament. Perhaps it is for this reason that the criticisms made concerning the academic bias of the course tend to be aimed only at the obvious target—the linguistic requirements, especially Hebrew. Perhaps this issue needs a psycho-analyst, rather than a theologian, to sort it out. It certainly seems to many, including some Biblical scholars, that the linguistic requirements do not produce results at all proportionate to the time and effort expended, and that that time and effort would be better spent elsewhere. But this is regarded by others as pandering to the student's laziness, and recently, from the school of Biblical Theology, which is still influential in Scotland, there has come a strong counter-attack against all modernizers, in which the demand for less Hebrew and Greek has been described as 'obscurantist'. Even those who make this demand would, however, deny strongly that they wish to lessen the intellectual demands of the course, and would use the time saved for more thorough study in theology and practical theology. The idea of a radically different type of training, less intellectual, more personal and experiential, has never been seriously considered, though it would seem to be what is appropriate to the warm-hearted, non-intellectual minister described above. The suggestion has been made that the Church should institute a residential college at which all its students would spend one year on the completion of their academic course, and where practical training, field work, devotional discipline and even personal analysis could be combined. This idea has had support from some theological professors who would like to see practical concerns banished altogether from the academic classrooms. It is highly questionable whether this splitting of the academic and the practical would be good for either. The suggestion may be significant because it illustrates the split-mind of the Scottish Church. A new realization of the importance of the practical, the human, the experiential; and a strong inheritance of Presbyterian intellectualism—and the two can not yet be integrated.

2 · THE REFORMED MINISTRY TODAY

The debate about the divinity curriculum will scarcely begin to clear until at least one prior question has been raised—the nature of the ministry, the respects in which it is still identical with the reformation doctrine, and the respects in which it has undergone change.

The intellectual bias of Reformed theology follows from its understanding of the Word. 'Faith cometh by hearing, and hearing by the Word of God.' This was the Reformers' own experience, and it became normative for the Church. The Reformed Church is a Church under continual reformation from the Word of God. This word is heard in the preaching of the gospel. 'The preaching of the Word of God is the Word of God.' It was possible to envisage the Christian good of Scotland as served, and the Church built up, as the people of Scotland were brought within the sound of preaching, through a territorial ministry and the exercise of discipline by the Kirk Sessions, and so were instructed, discipled or disciplined, in knowledge, obedience and faith. One might expect this to result in a clergy-ridden people, and the picture of little Calvins and Knoxes thundering and domineering in every Scottish parish is a popular myth. In fact, the success of this venture in Christian nurture seems to have resulted rather in a people-ridden clergy. When people have learned their catechism too well, and have mastered the definitions of dogma, they are apt to become sermon-tasters of the worst kind, judging the sermon by whether it says what they already know to be true, and quick to detect any deviation from accepted soundness of doctrine. It is often forgotten that it is possible to understand all mysteries, and not have charity.

We have moved very far from that situation today. The modern congregation does not claim any competence to judge the soundness of its minister's theology; rather it tends to assert its complete ignorance of all such matters. Many reasons can be adduced for the change. The theological clarity of the catechisms became arid and dry, and warmer evangelical movements brought in different and confusing influences; the rise of the denominations, and the end of the one-church-in-each-parish situation meant that the parish ceased to be the unit of church life; the congregation, and finally the individual soul, became the unit. Whatever the reasons, the prevalent attitude seems to be that we are 'ordinary Christians' and ordinary Christians know—and need to know—little of theology, or of the Bible for that matter. But they have needs, and they expect the minister to meet these needs. Perhaps it all stems from the great spell-binding preachers of the nineteenth century, with their utterly dependent congregations, perhaps there are more recent causes; but a 'psychological priesthood' (as it has been called) is a widespread attitude to the ministry. The main burden of the success and failure of the congregation (conceived by its members in terms of finance and numbers) is made to rest fairly and squarely on the shoulders of the minister. It is he who out of the store of his personality and gifts, in preaching and in prayer, in visiting, in organizing, in handling people, provides for their spiritual and religious needs, and keeps the congregation happy. When he does well the church fills, when he does badly the church empties. (What happens meantime to neighbouring congregations is another matter; church life of this kind is subtly competitive.) The minister is still expected to perform the traditional functions of preaching, visiting, conducting public worship, teaching, but because the criterion of success is a worldly one, the role-expectation has subtly changed, and the gifts most prized have little to do with theological education. A pleasing personality and a friendly manner may be valued more than spiritual insight; the gift of eloquence and the ability to produce good illustrations may matter more than 'rightly dividing the word of truth'. (The cult of the funny children's address is the nadir here, where it does not matter what heresy or platitude is propounded, so long as it is tagged on to an amusing story, or extracted from an ingenious object-lesson.) In public worship, the provision of what some Americans call 'meaningful worship experiences' can become an exercise in psychological manipulation far enough removed from the worship of the people of God. One might sum it up by saying that the traditional view of the ministry expects the minister to feed his people with bread; the modern view asks only circuses.

Admittedly one can exaggerate these tendencies (Bible and theology are not totally irrelevant to the modern congregation), and in any case they are distortions of genuine elements in the minister's relationship with his people (an unpleasing personality, and dullness in the pulpit, are not to be recommended), but it is important to recognize that these distortions are the cause of much frustration in the ministry and much of the confusion about theological education. Whatever be the minister's own convictions, he is under strong pressure from the congregation's role-expectation of him, but to fulfil these expectations he needs less of theological education and more of various skills unrelated to theology. The things in which he has been educated seem of little value, but will he ever be more than an amateur in those things in which he has not been educated? For there are experts in all these fields. The ad-man knows more about psychological manipulation, and the salesman is more skilled at getting decisions. The business executive can handle organization far more efficiently and smoothly. The psychotherapist understands the hidden motivations of individuals and groups, and is skilled at exorcising their fears and resolving their conflicts. The sociologist is able to understand the needs and the trends of the community (even to the answer to the question why they go, or don't go to church). The educationalist and the trained youth leader know much more about the young. Not unnaturally, the minister feels aggrieved that these techniques have not been prominent in his preparation for the ministry.

The most serious distortion which occurs when a minister accepts the role expected of him in a 'minister-centred church'[1] is in the relationship between minister and people. There is no longer mutual respect. The minister (on whom so much depends) is either idolized or criticized, and he for his part becomes the creature of his congregation endeavouring always to please them (cf. the stage parson, and the motto of the popular preacher, 'Give the people what they want and a little more of it than they expect') or else he despises them, for he knows how to handle them (cf. what one minister said to a divinity student before a service, 'I always soften them up at the beginning'). The minister today may have difficulty in establishing his authority (or finding wherein it consists), but he is readily accorded a certain apartness. It seems proper to treat as aspects of the 'psychological priesthood' two common views of the ministry —as exemplary and as representative. The minister is an example to the flock, of whom more is expected than of the ordinary church member, in standards of conduct and of devotion. A strange kind of innocence is sometimes expected too, as though there were some things he shouldn't know about. Above all, he is an example of dedication. He is the real Christian, who is serving God all the time. (It is sad to record that there are men who offer themselves as candidates for the ministry because they feel that they will not be fully dedicated to God until they take this step; but they are hardly to be blamed when the Church itself talks of the ministry as 'full-time service'.) And the minister is the representative. The Church is not considered to be present anywhere unless there is a minister. The Church in industry means ministers in factories. The Church in education means ministers taking the school assembly. The Church and politics means the minister on the platform. For those inside

[1]I am deliberately avoiding quotations and references in this essay, but must make grateful acknowledgment of the stimulation provided by two American books—the essay on 'The Christian Ministry' by Robert Clyde Johnson in the study material which he edited for the United Presbyterian Church in the USA., entitled *The Church and its Changing Ministry*, and the late H. Richard Niebuhr's *The Purpose of the Church and its Ministry*.

and outside, the dog-collar has become the Church's flag.

Much of what has been said above applies to the towns and cities. In the country parishes the sense of the congregation, its weal or woe, is less developed, but there the church tends to depend even more upon the minister, though more upon his presence than upon his gifts. He is there to provide the rites of passage for life's turning-points. He is available in time of need. He is the Church. One country minister has confessed that years of faithful and frequent visiting of his flock and parish seem only to have confirmed them in the belief that people join the Church in order to be cared for.

One obvious way of repudiating the 'psychological priesthood' view of the ministry is for the minister to assert his own authority on his own terms. One might expect this to happen oftener than it does—perhaps it begins oftener, but does not last. There are two main forms—the theological and the ritualist. Here the congregation is given the medicine that is good for them, whether they like it or not, and no attempt is made to sugar the pill. If they cannot understand the minister's sermons and find them dull, that is a sign of their unregenerate nature; if they dislike his new Order of Service, and his archaic and incomprehensible prayers, that is their vulgarity and lack of spirituality. Surely it is not for this either—to be little tin gods, or to say

I am Sir Oracle,
And when I ope my lips let no dog bark!

that men are called and educated for the ministry. The resemblance that this has to the authority of the Reformed pastor is only specious, for such a man has only achieved independence of his congregation, he has not achieved any unity with them.

The fundamental reason why these views of the ministry —psychological, dogmatic, or ritualistic clericalism—cannot satisfy us is because they all share in the same misunderstanding of the Church. The minister-centred church instead of being primarily a fellowship is primarily an institution, instead of being the people of God in the world it is the place apart from the world to which people repair for religious inspiration, truth and help. This kind of complaint about the Church is becoming familiar enough today. One of the earlier books by the Bishop of Woolwich is called *On Being the Church in the World,* and it is not a wild speculation to suggest that one reason why he and others are averse to the image of a 'God out there' is that it is the religion which corresponds to the reality of a 'Church out there'—a Church which seeks its God by turning its back on the world. The attack upon religion, and the appeal of 'religionless Christianity', has the same source. It is not even easy to know what we mean by the Church being 'in the world' today (we tend to use such phrases as slogans), because the world itself has become fragmented. The functions of work, of home (and neighbourhood) and of leisure are performed in different places, and with different people. But it is not difficult to see that the tendency has been for the Church (or 'religion') to become simply one of the leisure-time activities which people take up if they are, or become, interested in it. Religion may be an important resource for the living of daily life (one man said to his minister, 'We look to you to re-charge our batteries') but a Church in this stance exists—like any other club—primarily for the sake of its own members. Because these members, or some of them, give liberal and unselfish service to the Church the fact is obscured that the Church itself is self-centred, a corporate egotism. When such a congregation undertakes 'mission' it is more concerned to strengthen the congregation by the addition of good members, than constrained by love of the unlovely and the lost. (The lost are not always welcome.) Christian service is thought of exclusively as service to the Church; the Church's service to the world is something the ordinary Christian may support by liberality, prayers and interest, but his Christian work is what he does in his own congregation. Thus, as has been noted, the minister becomes the norm of the Christian, and active Christian service becomes a matter of 'supporting the minister' in the activities of the Church. But there is a limit to the amount of service that is needed around a Church, to keep the business of the congregation and its organizations going, and the range of gifts that is thus used is limited. The minister-centred church produces the 'ordinary Christian', for it does not encourage the church-members to stir up the gifts that are in them, or to rise to their full maturity in Christ. It keeps them rather in a position of dependence; and the minister's own position hangs on this. It is sometimes suspected that some ministers who complain about the lack of support in their congregations and parishes would be more than a little disappointed if it were proved that some part of the church's life could get along quite well without them.

The criticism that must be made of most of the demands for reform in the theological curriculum is that they aim to produce successful ministers for the minister-centred church. This is the reason why the academic is despised, and the demand is for techniques, methods, training. The minister must be equipped to be the successful full-time executive of this rather peculiar business. Until this view of the ministry is criticized a genuine modernizing of the course will not be possible.

Material for a more adequate view is already at hand in the movements of thought and life in the Church today. (If the pictures of church and ministry given above were exaggerations, caricatures, the other side of the picture will be suggested now.) For instance, it was once a characteristic of ecumenical discussion about the Church that it became always an argument about the ministry. Today, on the other hand, discussion about the ministry tends to locate itself within a discussion about the Church. The trouble with the view that 'the Church begins in a clergy' is that on that view it tends to end in a clergy too, and 'the place of the laity in the Church' becomes a subject for anxious discussion! Recently we have rather been reminded that whatever the differentiation of function within the Body of Christ, the word 'ministry' is used in the New Testament of the whole Church, and that the Ministry of Word and Sacrament can be rightly understood only in the context of that ministry in which the whole Church participates as the Body of Christ. The whole baptised community is called to an active response to the gospel, in worship, witness and service, in its corporate priesthood and in the diversity of individual gifts. Ministry in the Church (and here perhaps we should learn to think of elders, deacons, Sunday School teachers, organists, etc., as well as ministers of Word and Sacrament) is for the sake of the ministry of the Church, it is for edification, in the characteristic Pauline term, to 'build up' the Church. The text, Ephesians 4.11 and 12, on which Calvin based his doctrine of the ministry, can be read again in the light of modern discussion: 'And these were his gifts: some to be apostles, some prophets, some evangelists, some pastors and teachers, to equip God's people for work in his service, to the building up of the body of Christ.'

Many movements in the life of the Church seem to be expressing, or seeking, the same insight. The Layman's Movement, in its many forms, is seeking to enable the members to realize that they *are* the Church. The 'Tell Scotland Movement' reminds the Church that mission is the task of the whole Church, a continuing and corporate responsibility. The Kirk Weeks have thrown up a group of laymen vitally concerned about what it means to be the Church in the place of one's work, with all the ethical and theological perplexities that that concern entails. The Stewardship Movement calls men to stewardship of time and talents, as well as possessions. In some of the early campaigns in Scotland, congregations found that they could not use the offers of service which came flooding in; it requires only a limited number of people to tend the church garden, or take the flowers to the sick after the evening service. It soon became clear that a far wider conception of Christian service was needed. The movement of Adult Christian Education meets us at the point where we feel our inadequacy to these new demands, and helps men to equip themselves for witness and service. All these are little enough, and ineffectual enough, but they may be seen as signs of a movement of the spirit, by which the Church recovers its *raison d'être*, and remembers that it is (as William Temple said) 'the only society which exists primarily for the sake of those who are not its members'.

Therefore one sometimes hears it said that the laity are the Church's front-line troops, and that the ministry is simply there to support, supply and train them. This view may in the end be as dangerous a distortion as that which it supplants. Such an absolute distinction of function may lead to clericalism of a different kind. The Church cannot be so neatly divided. All Christians serve the world; all Christians serve one another. Yet the view that makes the minister the support of the laity seems nearer the truth than the reverse. But this view brings into prominence once more the traditional functions of the ministry, rather than the gimmicks and techniques on which much modernizing has concentrated. If this view is accepted, the key functions of the ministry are teaching and preaching, and the minister becomes the resource-person who helps the people to understand what it means to be the Church today, who out of his knowledge of theology and church history can throw light on the decisions which they must take, who can use all the resources of modern scholarship to help them to understand what the Word of God says to them today. It is not only the individuals who have to wrestle with the problems of faith and the demands of obedience; the congregation as a whole has witness to make and an obedience to render. Preaching is where the promise and command of the gospel are heard by minister and people together in their concrete situation. The meaning of this obedience has to be worked out in study group, in pastoral interview, in the courts and Committees of the Church. Since we live in a world with a high standard of general education, and since the problems of Christian faith and life in the modern world are very perplexing, if not unprecedented, there is need, as never before, of high intellectual standards in the ministry. Warm-heartedness without intelligence, kindness without imagination are not going to render the service which the Church most urgently requires.

Does this mean, then, that the theologian is the little Pope in each congregation, and that this is after all the modern solution to the problem of the ministry? This certainly appeals to an authoritarian mentality to which a certain type of theology also appeals, but it must be decisively rejected. It must be admitted, however, that it carries to the extreme point the intellectualism which has always been inherent in the Reformed view of the ministry. It requires therefore to be said today that if warm-heartedness without intelligence is not sufficient, neither is intelligence without warmth. It is noteworthy that if people have a choice between someone who is brilliant but cold, who speaks much but does not listen, and someone who is friendly but uninspiring, with little to say but a sympathetic ear, they will choose the second. Who will say that that is an unspiritual choice? The teaching and preaching, the leading and guidance which the minister is called to supply must be a loving service, not a domination of the congregation. The most serious objection to the minister-centred church was that it distorts the relationship between minister and congregation by destroying respect. Respect must be mutual. There are gifts and resources in the congregation as well as in the minister; the minister must be a learner and a listener as well as a teacher and a speaker. Theology does not provide ready-made answers that can be offered in a 'take it or leave it' manner, it is one of the resources that is brought to the problems of Christian faith and life. The people may teach the minister not only about the world (which they clearly will, if he can give them the confidence to speak frankly), but also about God; and the minister will not only teach them about God, he will also (to their surprise, perhaps) interpret the world to them, and help them to understand the pressures and movements and cultural forces with which they live. But it is as a theologian, as a man of the Word that he makes his specific contribution to this conversation.

It is usually assumed that a minister knows nothing about the world because he is a man of the Word, and has never earned his living in a factory. It is important to note that in this he is no different from a doctor, or a lawyer, or a schoolteacher. What is 'the world' of which the minister is ignorant? For the world today is not a single place, but many different places, and no one person can experience all possible worlds. Does the miner know the problems and pressures of working in a large department store? Does the motor mechanic understand the problems of the shipyard worker, or the blast-furnaceman the frustrations of the accountant? We all have limited experience. It seems to one returning to academic life after more than a decade in the ministry that he knows 'the world' quite differently from those whose career has been spent in one institution of higher learning after another—from public school to University, to research, to a lectureship, to a chair. A cloistered (but not a sinless) world! Experience, in human terms, is not simply a matter of where you have been, and what you have seen, but of how deeply you have seen, of your ability to use your imagination, to enter into and understand the lives and feelings of others. Where open relationships exist in the Church, experience is being widened all the time.

The unsolved problem is how to integrate the academic requirements, which must not be reduced (this may be said without prejudice to the question whether Hebrew and Greek really are essential tools for the exposition of Scripture), with the personal requirements of the modern ministry, the capacity for personal relationships, the wisdom and understanding of others that encourages their response to leadership, and learns from their refusals also. (The word patience has been deliberately avoided here, for patience can be the virtue of theological arrogance, waiting till the benighted at last see the light.) More could be done in the selection of candidates, where the Church of Scotland is much less thorough than the Church of England. It is hard to see how *agape*—for it is really Christian love that we are looking for—can be *taught*. A greater measure of corporate life might help, but many of us would be most unwilling to give up our exposed position in the centre of a University to become a seminary withdrawn from the world. This would be the very reverse of what we are asking the Church to do. Within the academic course the key may be in the way theology itself is taught and learned. Relationships between teacher and student may express freedom and respect, and point the way to fruitful relationships later on—or they may express the authoritarianism that destroys relationships. There can be no sure recipe for something so personal as this. At one level what is required is the measure of self-understanding, awareness of one's own hidden needs and fears, that enables a man to deal charitably with others. Perhaps this is the real task of 'spiritual discipline', if an appropriate form could be found.

In a time such as ours, of rapid social change, adaptability and the capacity to make intelligent experiment are of the greatest importance. For this reason practical training must be subordinate to, and held in close connection with practical theology. Practical training answers the question, *How* to do the job? Practical theology asks the prior question, *What* is it that we are aiming to do? The Church needs not technicians, i.e., men trained to perform certain skills, but designers, i.e., men qualified to judge when to scrap the old machines, and able to apply their theories to the production of more effective ones. It is also of little profit if in one class men learn to think critically about preaching, and then go for training to someone who tries to teach them how to produce what they believe is the wrong kind of sermon.

The minister must know more than theology. How much more, and what precisely, is a different question. Originally the Arts degree provided a broad general education. Today specialization begins in the schools, and men come to the study of theology from a variety of degree courses, some of them quite narrow in their content. Since this is a scientific age, perhaps it is a good thing that many of these are scientists. Does it not then matter what you study so long as you study *something* before you do theology? This seems an odd doctrine, though some people appear to hold it. With the introduction of a first-degree in theology in two of the Scottish Universities, the Church may feel it necessary to re-state or re-define its requirements. It is unlikely that it will encourage young men to begin theological studies straight from school: whether this is conservatism or wisdom is hard to tell.

It may be that the day for 'broad general education' is past, and that the important thing for the theologian is to understand these disciplines that border on his own, and to enter into conversation with them. The different branches of theological study have their own neighbours—the historian, the philosopher, the philologist, the archaeologist, the psychologist, the sociologist—and in the pastoral ministry there is scope for conversation with the doctor, the social worker, the teacher. There are signs today that groups which overcome professional isolation are welcomed, and though they bring their own tensions, they bring also a new view of one's own function and place in society. In a broader way, the Church itself, as is suggested above, may be the place where mutual education takes place, as members share with each other their experience of 'the world', and learn to look at the world together. Here the daily newspaper, television, and modern novels, drama, films, music, art, have their part in the conversation. (Why are church groups so philistine? Church dramatic clubs perform English country-house comedies of the most escapist 'snob' kind, and are afraid that serious modern drama might offend the congregation. Church groups study the Bible, but would never dream of linking that with *Lord of the Flies*, or *Billy Liar*.)

Much could be done towards the integration of courses in a faculty. In one college, students have had five different courses on Luther. In spite of the Church's conservatism, and the pressure of those who believe that revelation is given in a particular language, the time must come when at least one of the biblical languages is optional. But even the time thus saved would be too little for the provision of additional courses, such as are often desired. There seems to be wisdom in the decision to provide intensive residential courses in the probationary year, when experience in the ministry has made certain questions urgent and alive. The logical continuation of this is that the courses and conferences for ministers, which some of the Faculties and some of the Committees of the Church already hold, must be extended and become part of the normal life of the Church. The Scottish minister still refers to the room where he works as his 'study', not his 'office'. It is important, if the Church is to be faithfully served, that it should continue to be so.

III

The Free Churches

ROBIN SHARP

1 · INTRODUCTION

THE *Observer* not so long ago published a series of highly controversial articles on the image of the parson today. The typical Free Church minister emerged from that enquiry by Paul Ferris as first and foremost a preacher, a preacher in an era when the sermon has lost its magic spell and the chapels stand three-quarters empty in the land. It is patent that the Free Churches face a dilemma.[1] Seduced from their original vocations by the garish popularity of the nineteenth century they are not what they used to be in any sense. To blame this onto the ministry in general or theological training in particular, as people are prone to do from time to time, is grossly unfair. If there is a crisis it is a crisis for the whole Church. By and large the Church gets the ministry it deserves. The colleges cannot force upon the Churches a ministry they do not want. On the other hand, if the Churches have a mind to renew their life, as they are beginning to do, then training for the ministry becomes quite crucial. Frustration arises chiefly when it is seen that the colleges are equipping their students not to pioneer a new situation but to keep the wheels of the old one turning.

'Is he an acceptable preacher?' is the question usually asked by Methodist circuit stewards about a minister whom they are thinking of inviting. Preaching 'with a view' among the Baptists and Congregationalists indicates that this is still

[1]Brilliantly set out by Christopher Driver in *A Future for the Free Churches?* (SCM Press, 1962).

the main criterion Free Churchmen employ in assessing a minister's worth. Pastoral gifts, described as 'being a good visitor', are also desiderated along with the ability to get on with the various groups—Sunday School, youth club, women's meetings and so on—which make up a congregation's life. If a man is good at 'efforts' and his wife is 'a good worker', then what more could be desired? The successful minister, such as may be found in the church-going ribbon of suburbia and the coastal retiring places, is a man with a minister-centred, organization-dominated church energetically fostering its own fellowship and only marginally involved in the secular community of its neighbourhood. He is the relatively well-paid servant of his congregation's religious needs, paramount among which is the desire to be cushioned against the pressures of contemporary society. Although it is recognized that many church tasks are the layman's job, it is the minister who shares them out and who must approach people to persuade them to take them on. So he is the chief organizer, the man who ties all the ends together and who is finally answerable for what happens.

No college staff would accept such a conception of the ministry themselves, let alone train men explicitly for it. Yet the subtle pressures of what people expect, together with a lack of any clear criticism from the colleges of this popular 'theology of the Church' make it inevitable that the overall direction of the present system is towards maintaining the *status quo*. The aim of theological training as now practised might be said to be providing the matter for preaching plus an attempt to supply techniques for running a successful church. This is no mean task and without being presumptuous we may judge that it is in large measure being fulfilled. Before turning to some suggestions for fresh thinking we must look at what is now being done in the Free Church colleges in England and Wales.

2 · SELECTION AND TRAINING TODAY

No systematic information seems to exist on this topic, though a series of articles in the *Expository Times* in 1962 and 1963 threw some light on the various procedures employed. For what follows I am indebted to report forms which came back somewhat spasmodically to my own office and to a memorandum prepared by the Secretary of the recently formed Consultative Committee on Training for the Ministry of the British Council of Churches. Incidentally it should be noted that we make a very dismal job of interpreting the colleges to lay members of the Church. The aura of mystique which surrounds them is quite absurd. Coupled with the evangelical suspicion that training is beside the point this creates a real need for the kind of illustrated brochure or pamphlet issued by CACTM for the Church of England.[1]

Selection methods are largely shaped by the pattern of the various Churches. Among Baptists and Congregationalists candidates go with a commendation from their own church before a county union or association committee and then before a college selection committee with a written examination. No minimum academic requirements are prescribed by Baptist colleges but most Congregational colleges ask for university or faculty entrance qualifications. The Presbyterian Church of England selects students through local presbytery committees and the Church Candidates Board. Men under 25 are expected to do a degree and then take a college entrance exam in which New Testament Greek is included (Hebrew too until recently). A Methodist candidate must first be a qualified local preacher, an attainment involving written and oral examinations and a 'trial' sermon as well as regular preaching. He must then be

[1]The annual reports of the Methodist Ministerial Training Department have improved radically in format recently but as official documents they go only part-way to meet the need.

approved by his local circuit, take nationally set examinations, be examined by a district synod committee and then by the synod itself, meanwhile preach two local sermons in circuits other than his own, submit a written sermon and finally be examined by the Candidates Committee of the Methodist Conference. The judgment on his fitness to enter college is given by the Ministerial Session of the Conference, a body with over three hundred voting members. There is no evidence that this lengthy procedure produces better ministers than the other Churches, though it may have the advantage of allowing a man to consider the question of his call gradually over a whole year. Perhaps the comments of Parkinson might be invited! The academic minimum is now four G.C.E. passes which can be waived in special cases. It can easily be seen that the Free Churches have a wide variety of academic standards ranging from the Presbyterians who take only graduates to Methodists and Baptists who take perhaps only 15 per cent with degrees.

Fear of an over-academic ministry is legitimate and we cannot limit the area of vocation by a simple intellectual rule of thumb. But in an age when higher education is mushrooming it must be obvious that some of our proportions have gone wrong.

The major Free Church denominations have between them 23 colleges in England and Wales. Breaking this down, the Methodists have 6 colleges with a total of roughly 300 students, the Congregationalists with 8 colleges have about 195, the Baptists 7 colleges for 200 students, and the Presbyterians 2 for 50. Without exception all are within range of university cities and some men in every college are working for a theological degree. The vast majority are fully residential, though by no means full of theological residents. In Wales, however, there are one or two places where libraries bequeathed by venerable preachers seem to have priority over accommodation for students. A separate chapel is near universal, though again there are places where it doubles with the college library. The principal's house is usually closely attached but other members of staff often live some way off which makes for a certain lack of the kind of community found in an Anglican college. This may not be altogether a bad thing, since it is the natural result of having a married staff. Numbers of students range from 5 to 75. Most college buildings date from the last century but even John Betjeman could hardly be expected to enthuse over them.

In the typical way of all things British the length of training is subject to an almost infinite number of variations. The Congregationalists in true independent style have the most; according to your college you may do a degree plus three, two or one year's training (which may or may not include a theological degree) or you may do a non-graduate course of varying length. As a Methodist you spend two or three years doing a degree, or diploma or college course plus an optional extra year of practical training. In a Baptist college the basic course for a degree or diploma is three years which may be preceded or followed by a one year course of varying nature. Presbyterians do three years, always including a degree. In all denominations men above student age have shorter courses—and it must not be forgotten that Methodists are the only one of the four denominations not to have women students in their colleges.

Every theological college principal is acutely aware of a pressure upon him to include more and more subjects in the curriculum. But there is no similar pressure to throw subjects out. As in medicine, the last hundred years have witnessed a tremendous growth in complexity in the subject matter of theology as well as the evolution of numerous sciences and philosophies which bring the traditional subject matter under disturbing scrutiny. If a college teaches only the traditional recipe—Old Testament, New Testament, Church History, Systematic Theology, Pastoralia and Preaching—it could be quite irrelevant and out of date. If on the other hand it tries to do the old stuff plus courses in all the relevant modern disciplines, its training period will get longer and longer and it will be a remarkable student who survives to the end. We are waiting for someone somewhere to cut the Gordian Knot, but so far, in vain.

Meanwhile the staple diet of the Free Church colleges remain the old formula just described. Whether or not students are following a degree course the subjects are taught academically. Almost all will learn some Greek, and some must do Hebrew. For those not linguistically gifted this is a wearisome and dispiriting chore. Quite apart from this linguistic work, this means, in the Old Testament for example, a considerable study of the literary and historical background of a book and of its sources—J, E, D and P and so on. It also involves a knowledge of the references in the text. Thus, supposing Isaiah was a set book for an exam, a student would be invited to comment on a phrase like 'Call his name Mahershalalhashbaz'. To do well he would not only have to explain the meaning of this strange term but set it in its context in the book. Now we obviously don't want a ministry cut off from our holy book, so that much of it becomes nothing more than mumbo-jumbo. On the other hand how sensible is it to try to get men to remember a mass of odd facts of this kind when they are all accessible in first-class commentaries? They must know how to use commentaries critically and how to tell a good one from a bad one, which will involve some detailed textual study. But far too much time is now spent on learning 'gobbets' or what six different commentators make of a famous crux (e.g., Mark 4.12 where Jesus appears to say that he used parables to conceal what he said). So there is little opportunity for thinking about what it all means for us today. If we can explain the sources of the Pentateuch and label every verse with one of the famous letters, so what? Why should we bother to read it still? Are the Joseph stories anything more than historical romance? What about the plagues, and so on? The trouble is that courses dominated by university degree syllabuses are not designed to raise basic questions of belief and relevance. The presupposition of much current study is admirable enough—to interpret for today you must understand what a passage meant in its original context. This delivers us from the bandying-about of isolated texts, but too often the emphasis on original meaning is so great that the student never gets round to thinking about contemporary application.

Much the same applies to the teaching of Church History. There is a corpus of knowledge to be acquired, not an approach to be imparted. Just as secular history used to be thought of as kings and battles, so church history seems to be composed of heresies and schisms, bishops and theologians.[1] The relation between 'secular' and ecclesiastical history is seldom established, nor is there much attempt to discover what it was like to be an ordinary church member in say eighth-century Spain or seventeenth-century Germany. There is also an alarming tendency in Protestant circles to regard the period A.D. 450-1517 as a totally dark age for the Church, and to be quite ignorant about the life of this period in East and West. History is a powerful propaganda weapon for religious denominations no less than nation states and it is only in the last few years that it has been possible to obtain relatively objective accounts of the Reformation both on the Continent and in Great Britain.[2] How sympathetically do English Free Churchmen study the history of the Book of Common Prayer, the Caroline divines and the Oxford Movement, let alone counter-reformation Catholicism and Eastern Orthodoxy?

In Systematic Theology there is a scheme to be established —the doctrine of God, of man, of Christ, of the Church and of the last things. Heresies are exposed and orthodoxy is vindicated. Too often, though, theology is answering its own questions and establishing an elaborate system which is divorced from contact with existential concerns. One dilemma which faces the teacher of systematics is how to use the

[1] I owe this point and a number of others to the Rev. Donald Knighton of Droitwich.

[2] *The Reformation* by Owen Chadwick in the Pelican History of the Church (1964) is an admirable example of the new approach.

work of the masters—Augustine, Thomas, Luther and Barth. Do you give a potted version of one or more systems (or someone else's potted version) or do you encourage men to read parts of their work—and that of secular thinkers—at first hand? The latter may be difficult but it is infinitely more stimulating; summaries somehow always manage to suppress the vital spark of the original. This approach may not give men a very clear-cut system, but it should produce a flexible approach. If theology was thus taught the most recent modern texts would be studied equally with the old. One of the most depressing features of the *Honest to God* episode has been the parson's inability to cope with the discussion at the local level. Again and again one hears of ministers failing almost completely to exploit a situation when laymen seriously wanted to discuss theological questions. One can only conclude that they did not receive the proper equipment during their training.

Added to this basic curriculum is a larger or smaller number of ancillary courses. Among these the two universal subjects are preaching and pastoralia. I think ministers would give general testimony that the former is much better done than the latter. The weekly sermon class and voice production lesson are standard features and preaching is the main out-of-college activity for most Free Church students. As well as giving experience, preaching in surrounding churches, which usually pay a fee, helps to supplement grants. There are some colleges where the men are conducting two services every Sunday of the term and in vacation too. Methodists are of course local preachers when they reach college, so this is not altogether a new experience for them. One wonders however how many people manage to combine with their preaching the thinking in which their course is involving them and how many simply keep the two realms in watertight compartments.

Part of the difficulty is that when they leave college almost all students go to be full ministers of churches whose congregations are not anxious to be guinea pigs for novice preachers. If the Free Churches decided to make the first year or two out of college a continuation of training, with the student as an assistant minister, the experience of preaching could be gained then. This would allow the college to give more time to basic training and a discussion of contemporary methods of communication. At present a student is existentially committed to the familiar pattern of producing two twenty-minute addresses for every Sunday (he will not of course make new ones every time) before he has the chance to work out whether this is really what is needed. The colleges should be a laboratory to test not simply competence at performing the traditional functions but the functions themselves. There is a natural fear of new-fangled ideas and jejeune experiments but it is surely much more frightening to see the living forms of the Church's life becoming ossified and progressively detached from ordinary modes of thinking and communication.

Pastoralia as its name implies is a collection of subjects relating to the pastoral ministry. It is frequently both studied and taught without much enthusiasm. The teacher may be primarily an academic with little experience of the local church, and the students do not see the problems as immediately pressing. Certain things are always included—visiting, counselling, interviewing for baptisms and weddings, the conduct of worship and the administration of the sacraments, church administration and law, the legalities of marriage, etc. You might describe these as the minister's professional know-how. It is a well-worn cliché that all this can only be learned properly in experience—but not in the unaided and unguided experience which is the lot of most newly ordained ministers. So much depends upon the approach and experience of the teacher in determining the depth and range of pastoral training in college. It is clear that much greater use could be made of good local ministers to give regular courses in this field. At present there is little systematic teaching about the rapidly developing social services of the welfare state, so that the student is quite unaware of either the services or insights they have to offer.[1]

When we leave these traditional pastures we find colleges providing everything or nothing. The selection any college makes will relate both to the length of its course and to staff available. There are few where all students will tackle more than one or two extra subjects. If we list the courses now available somewhere it may at any rate indicate the impossibility of simply adding modern specialisms to the traditional basis. They include—denominational history and principles, practical work, industrial and hospital courses, philosophy, ecumenical studies, Christian sociology, the welfare state, educational studies, general and pastoral psychology, marriage guidance, the devotional life, ethics, philosophy of religion and economics. It is ironic to reflect that the special skills I found myself requiring immediately on going into circuit ministry were driving a car and operating a cinema-projector, neither of which I had learned in college!

Quite apart from the question of pastoral training for students a matter requiring really serious attention in Free Church colleges is that of the pastoral care of the students themselves. 'It is sometimes assumed that when a person enters the portals of a theological college he leaves his spiritual problems behind him. All too often pastors are left pastorless while in training.'[2] As previously mentioned, Free Church colleges in general contrast strongly with Anglican colleges in lack of community sense. If there is a sense of community it is a student community, not one shared by staff and students alike. The result is that the college chairman has to become a mediator between the principal and the students on a gamut of matters ranging from minor variations in college worship to reconsideration of the

[1] A Report on 'Training for the Pastoral Office' adopted by the Methodist Conference of 1962, would, if implemented, meet many of the present deficiencies, but it makes no recommendations about the kind of staff or about co-operation with the functionaries of the welfare state.

[2] Keith R. Bridston, *Theological Training in the Modern World* (WSCF, 1954), p. 32.

whole curriculum. Frequently the tone of the student community, focused on a daily meeting, is very immature through trying to avoid being pious, and my own experience of many colleges in Britain forces me to concur with a remark of Dr John H. S. Kent of Manchester, that 'the internal failure of our colleges is a failure in tone.'[1] There is a strange stiffness about relationships which ought to be quite foreign to a small Christian community such as a college. It is this which inhibits pastoral care and though the appointment of a chaplain might help, what is really needed is a change of atmosphere.

It need hardly be said that the period of theological training often puts a great strain on a man. He becomes familiar through analytical study with what previously has been received with religious reverence. Thus his faith is under test precisely through his study and he knows that if he loses faith he cannot proceed with his vocation. A tension can develop between what is expected of him by the Church and his own internal evolution of thought and feeling. For a man in such a position a contemporary theological college is not exactly a therapeutic community. And yet we expect a minister to teach his church to be an accepting, loving and healing community when he has experienced so little of this in college. There are, of course, some glorious exceptions to this as to every other generalization in this chapter, but the problem is too serious to be glossed over.

Common worship is a central feature of community life and here the basic pattern is morning and evening prayers in chapel each weekday. Because so many students are away preaching there is not usually any service in college on a Sunday and those in residence will attend a local church. The form of daily worship bears some relation to denominational tradition in that there is no fixed outline or responsive prayers. A typical pattern is Bible reading, hymn and prayer, including the Lord's prayer. This may be all right for a few

[1]In an unpublished memorandum.

days but when it is followed out day after day it becomes profoundly unsatisfactory and highlights one of the major weaknesses in Free Church life. It is frequently though not always led by a student and as the tradition of extempore prayer lives on the congregation are often subjected to a characteristic poverty of language and lack of insight which makes corporate prayer extremely difficult. Little attempt is made to use the richness of the Christian liturgical heritage or to develop new forms. One might have thought that the freedom of college life in a free tradition would have encouraged the use of experimental daily prayers like those of the Taizé Community, but as in so many other ways freedom has become a worse tyrant than authority. There are, however, one or two colleges where a sustained attempt is being made to sing the psalms regularly to the new settings of Gelineau and Samson. Holy Communion is celebrated two or three times a term or once a week. This is probably more frequently than in the past and is to be welcomed. How often, though, does the manner of celebrating communion reflect the new insights of the liturgical movement, which can hardly be described as new-fangled? If students are not made familiar with these in college, when else are they going to get the chance, since on leaving they will immediately be involved in conducting services themselves every Sunday except when on holiday? The reluctance of colleges to experiment responsibly is deeply regrettable since the result is that some men will never experiment at all while others will do so without any guidance whatever as to basic principles.

Training for the ministry, as Canon Moss has so rightly pointed out[1] consists of three main stages—pre-college, college and post-college. Post-college training can be considered under two aspects—in-service training along the lines of the Anglican curacy system, and studies arranged by denominational authorities. Though Baptist colleges are beginning to experiment with one-year apprenticeship schemes, only the Methodist Church among those we are consider-

[1]*Clergy Training Today*, pp. 69 ff.

ing, has an established system. Without going into all the technicalities this means that after leaving college a man has to do two or three years in circuit ministry as a 'probationer' before proceeding to ordination. Although he has pastoral charge of one or more congregations he is much more closely under the authority and direction of the superintendent minister than an ordained minister. Officially the superintendent will train him in many practical aspects of the ministry, but if the probationer lives several miles away time and distance make this nearly impossible. A recent report on Probationers' Training recognized this and recommended the abolition of this type of situation. The trouble is that the probationer is still used as a cheap minister by many circuits and the weakness of Methodist strategy has been exposed by the fact that the recommendation has not been made mandatory.[1]

A new system of studies for probationer ministers is just getting under way. The idea is to change the accent from biblical and theological examinations to an essay system worked in conjunction with selected local ministers acting as tutors. All probationers now have an annual residential conference on a district basis—called a 'retreat' for some strange reason. These can be really valuable and it is to be hoped that the system will gradually be extended to more senior ministers. Training is never complete and when we consider the fantastic developments in society and theology since many men left college it is unthinkable that refresher courses should not be regarded as essential.

3 · SOME SUGGESTIONS FOR RENEWAL

The discussion on theological training which has been conducted in a variety of books and journals in recent years

[1]The usual rule of thumb for a difficult situation—either of advance or retreat—is, 'We want a minister; if we cannot afford that we'll have a probationer; if we can't pay for a probationer we'll have a deaconess; and if we can't afford a deaconess we'll have a caravan mission!'

is comprehensively referred to by Canon Herklots. This essay may best serve its purpose if we try to take the discussion one stage further. A large number of piecemeal suggestions have been made which nevertheless fail to give an overall pattern for what is admittedly a very complex problem. If we now offer a series of comprehensive suggestions it is not because of any conviction that they contain *the* solution, but merely that discussion of piecemeal reforms never gets to the root of the matter. It would be foolish to imagine that either the Churches or the colleges as a whole are likely to adopt the kind of radical experiment to be advocated. Unless one or two colleges do something which involves almost a death and resurrection, the good intentions of the moderate reformers—many in the colleges themselves—will continue to be fatally blurred by the weight of the traditional heritage. I greatly admire the spirit in which Canon Herklots writes and sympathize with his plea for gradual reform, but my conviction remains that this approach is unlikely to produce any decisive change in the atmosphere.

What is the Ministry of the Church today?

Surely any reform in the Church needs to be guided by a fundamental theological principle if it is to be of lasting worth. This applies to liturgy, architecture, organization and most of all to theological training. A college must have some overarching concept of the purpose of Church and ministry today within which many detailed experiments can be pursued. Nothing is more debilitating than a series of new projects which have no common direction, and it is against this which conservative spirits so rightly protest. Theology is in one sense always arbitrary and *ad hoc* and I make no pretence here of justifying a theology of the Church. It is, however, quite clear that the dominant note of our thinking about the Church today is service. This goes for Pope John, the Archbishop of Canterbury, Professor Hromadka, the Bishop of Woolwich, the New Delhi Assembly, the SCM and just about every church statement one can think of.

Jesus is the Servant Lord and the Church is called to enter into his Servant ministry. Albert van den Heuvel has described the hymn of Philippians 2.5-11 as 'the Magna Charta of the Church's calling'.[1] The Church is to be present in the world and to serve it. It does not exist for its own sake but for that of others. Its *raison d'être* is in giving itself for the life of the world. There is a danger here that Jesus the Servant may be distorted into Jesus the door-mat. We need to remember how troublesome Peter found Jesus' service to be.

Once we accept this charter for the Church—and it should not be forgotten that the old theology of the gathered Church and the new theology of the remnant Church being advocated by Fr Martin Thornton decisively reject it—we are in a position to see the function of a specially trained ordained man within it. To call him a minister is basically misleading since it suggests that the service of the Church is focused in him and chiefly executed by him. The function of the ordained man is to have representative responsibility for three distinctive actions of the Church through which its mission and ministry is performed. These are worship, proclamation and pastoral care—in all of which the love of Christ is to be made concrete in human lives. His special responsibility in these three spheres of activity is to equip and build up the whole body of the Church to serve in the world. To take the mission of the Church seriously in our post-Christian society means a radical re-orientation of the way in which all three activities are conducted. This cannot be done unless the way in which they are imparted in theological training is radically changed. Unless our theological convictions affect our manner of being ministers and thus, '*a priori*', of training ministers we shall simply be guilty of hypocrisy.

In a speech to the SCM Conference on 'The Death of the Church' in January 1964.

The Content of the Course

We envisage a college course of three or four years which will be equally relevant to the graduate in theology and the factory technician. Its basic content will be the Christian revelation in history with an emphasis on contemporary history. There will be no attempt to cover the whole of church history, or doctrine or the Bible except in the barest outline. Instead there will be a study in depth of a number of situations using at the same time all the available tools of historical and literary science together with the insights of sociology, psychology and the contemporary world view. Thus work on Genesis 1-11 will involve the use of a major commentary like von Rad's, the work of recent archaeologists such as Parrot, a discussion of the place of myth in human culture, the theory of evolution, the question of guilt and original sin, racial theories and so on. It is not much use knowing about Wellhausen's theory of the literary sources and Babylonian creation myths if we have no idea about the value of the Hebrew creation story for ourselves. While there is hardly any limit to the studies one could pursue arising out of these chapters, surely our training is not really up to scratch unless it brings students as forcefully into contact with Freud, Jung, Darwin and Huxley as with German professors of Old Testament. If we take a minor prophet we are immediately face to face with the question of Church and State, the Christian and politics, the Church in Eastern Europe, BCC statements on the bomb or African affairs, Canon Collins and Donald Soper. These matters are not mere periphera to be discussed by interested students in the common rooms but major problems deeply affecting the life of the Church.

Such illustrations could be multiplied indefinitely but it will already be clear that we reject the simple addition of a host of modern specialisms and techniques to the traditional subjects whether in a fourth year or in a series of special courses. This merely produces schizophrenia. Instead we are suggesting that the traditional quartet of the two Testaments, church history and theology be taught in the light of our contemporary understanding of the world. This means the rejection of the academic approach, however simplified, in favour of an applied or technological approach. Relevance and application must come before knowledge for its own sake. No one could care less about the names of the kings of Israel except the authors of a biblical quiz, but obedience to secular authority is a matter of life and death for many millions of our fellow Christians.

Dr John Kent in the memorandum referred to above has a perceptive critique for some current attempts to reform training. He writes, 'The weakness of the theory of ministerial training in recent years has been a tendency to feel that all that was needed to put things right was the inclusion of fresh subjects in the curriculum. Before the war psychology had a vogue which is now paralleled by that of sociology.'[1] Courses in the philosophy of science are seen as the answer to the problem of apologetics; a rash of sexual sensationalism produces a demand for courses in ethics; the decline in the power of the minister over his flock has led to the new enthusiasm for counselling (really amateur psychiatric fiddling) so that the parson can compete with the doctor and the lawyer, and so on. A lecture course in everything adds up to a knowledge of nothing, with the added danger that the ordinand thinks he "knows about" psychology, philosophy, ethics, counselling and the philosophy of science.'

How might a reshaped curriculum look in outline? John Kent has produced a scheme merely for purposes of discussion which does suggest how a new approach might be implemented:

'*First project*—intensive grounding in worship—practice —experiment—local varieties, etc.

[1]In *Bachelor of Divinity* (New York: Association Press, 1963) Walter Wagoner deals wittily with this theme in the course of an account of the present American ferment on training for the ministry.

Second project—the ministry in the modern world—again including study of local ministers and types of ministry.
Third project—the Church in the world—ecumenical theology and history, etc.
Fourth project—the meaning and authority of the Bible today, involving the history of criticism and modern discussion of revelation.
Fifth project—theology—the present crisis, its history and nature.
Sixth project—communication, preaching, evangelism—with possible set pieces, examination of local examples.
Seventh project—pastoralia—again historically, theologically, biblically—local research, etc.
Eighth project—the gospel in action in the modern world—ethics—local research.

Behind this, in the First Year men would do the Gospels and Acts (probably in English), in the Second Year the Pauline Epistles, and in the Third Year the remainder of the New Testament.' Apart from the obvious criticism that the Old Testament seems to have been forgotten completely, the main objection to this approach is that it would not give ordinary students a solid grounding in the traditional teaching of the Church. Yet what does the grounding currently imparted really achieve except to give ordinands a generally conservative outlook on things? It is extremely difficult to judge how much one is actually making use of the training one has received in any particular situation and background is obviously important, but I doubt whether I was using more than about 10 per cent of what I learned at college during the two years I spent in circuit.[1] I hardly ever had cause to refer to my essays or lecture notes, except for probationers' examinations. Faced with a church membership course, a baptismal instruction, a house-church or a young wives' group, knowledge of the Donatist schism or six scholars' views about the meaning of the Greek verb

[1]Though personally I found reading the Cambridge Theological Tripos highly stimulating.

ēngizo (lit. 'to be at hand') in Mark 1.15 is not much use. As long as the training can convince students of the fundamental nature of Christian revelation and experience in history, the amount of knowledge they receive is secondary. What they will not be taught out of college is the method of applying the revelation—if they have learned something about that and know where to look for their information, that will be enough.

It is not really possible to go into the detail of a curriculum outside a situation where it could be worked out in practice. Perhaps a few tentative thoughts on weekly themes within one of the suggested projects might not be out of place. If we take the first project which concentrates on worship, then quite apart from the basic experience of participation in the worshipping life of the college, this might start with an examination of the current practice of a particular denomination. That would lead to an investigation of its development and origins and link onto the mainstream history of Christian worship. Biblical evidence would then come under scrutiny and criteria for Christian worship and liturgical reform could be established. Music and architecture would be involved at all stages and the relation between public worship and private prayer discussed. There would be an opportunity to look at the tradition of other Christian bodies, through attendance at their worship and specially invited speakers. Finally the problems of worship in a secular age and the psychology of worship would be studied. There would also be experiments in devising forms of worship for a variety of situations and instruction in how to conduct the current forms we have in a living and vital way.

Another interesting idea for totally reshaping the curriculum has been worked out at Valparaiso University, a Lutheran institution in Northern Indiana.[1] The head of

[1]For what follows I am indebted to an article by Jerome Taylor in *Commonwealth* (Vol. LXXI 18), 29th Jan. 1960.

the religious department and instigator of the new courses, Pastor Robert W. Bertram, writes:

> The new courses reflect a deliberate effort to relate classroom instruction dynamically to the concrete problems and opportunities of the Christian life. Each week's reading assignment in the first and second years takes its departure from the Gospel and Epistle lections of that week. To this traditional biblical literature the student is now invited to take a second closer look and to explore its significance for himself and his world through socratically conducted classroom discussions, through supplementary reading in the Christian classics and even in recent fiction and through weekly essays. Moreover the same Christian themes which pervade the week's work in the classroom are echoed liturgically in the daily chapel services.

The article continues:

> Let us look for example at the syllabus entry for the 15th Sunday after Pentecost. Here the Gospel Lection concerns the Lord's raising from death of the only son of the widow of Nain (Luke 7.11-17). The methodological goal was 'Basic treatment of a miracle story as a revelation of Christ's victory over sin'. The doctrinal theme was 'Death as man's natural condition and Christ's work as the conquest of death'.
>
> During the previous week students had studied material on the synoptic Gospels in A. M. Hunter's *Introducing the New Testament*, together with Martin Luther's 'Explanation of the First Commandment' from the Lutheran Larger Catechism. Now they were asked to read and consider the first three chapters of Genesis, Psalm 89 (90) and the formulary for the confession of sins in the Lutheran service book. They were also asked to use a concordance of the Bible to look up and study other scriptural uses of the terms 'visit' and 'visitation'. (The account of the raising of the young man of Nain, it will be recalled, concludes with the statement that the beholders were struck with a great fear and 'glorified God, saying: A great prophet is risen up among us: and, God hath visited his people'.)

On the basis of their study, students were asked to write three essays in answer to the following questions: 1. Why does God's visitation in Jesus Christ fill the people with fear? 2. What clues do the first three chapters of Genesis afford as to the legitimate foundations of such fear? 3. Do Christians today meet Christ as did the young man of Nain? Where? When? How?

I would not for a moment suggest that this scheme is adequate for theological training or that the present set of lections—Roman, Anglican, or otherwise—provide a sufficiently wide range of basic material. Its value is to indicate that a fresh approach to the usual system of lecture courses is not only possible but practical.

The Method of Teaching

Closely allied to any revision of the content of the course is the method of teaching. In the memorandum already referred to Dr Kent writes: 'The role of the tutors seems to me to be twofold. First they should decide how their subjects help to illustrate and explicate the particular subject of the term, doing this in joint consultation, and teach as a group. Second, since they would almost certainly teach less in each term than they do now, they would be free to organize the seminar/tutorial teaching which is extremely difficult under the present system. The emphasis would be on dialectical teaching.' Though such a course is less academic it is not less intellectually rigorous. Pastor Bertram comments, 'This approach requires of the instructor that, far from being merely an academician, he bears a heightened pastoral responsibility for his students' spiritual maturity. The scientific quality of the doctrinal content suffers no diminution, indeed is enhanced by their pastoral orientation. Where personal relevance, where the life of the student is at stake, the importance of rigorous exactitude in formulation and of adequacy in communication becomes crucial.'[1]

[1]It relates to a course in Religious Education

Much greater use could be made of the type of teaching in use in many teacher-training colleges, as Canon Moss so rightly points out.[1] Small-group work, research projects, and one long essay per term would naturally find their place in the kind of scheme outlined.

The methods of course are not simply to be adopted because they are currently being employed in other educational institutions, though it is folly to be unaware of what is going on. The seminar/discussion method is crucial to our understanding of the task of the ministry today which cannot be effective if it assumes an authoritarian and superior status. That is not to suggest that there is no gospel to be proclaimed but that proclamation itself has to be carried on as much through dialogue and listening as by direct speaking. Incidentally this point is most persuasively argued by Canon Max Warren in his recent book *Perspective in Mission*[2] in connection with the Christian approach to other religions. The book also contains an excellent chapter on the handling of the missionary perspective in theological training.[3] If the minister is to be part of the team ministry of the whole Church and equip laymen for their mission in the world, he must learn in college what it means to search for truth openly and be part of the learning group. What Canon Moss writes from an Anglican position applies to the Free Churches: 'The person who today attempts to fulfil that ministry simply according to tradition finds the strain increasingly intolerable. The old monarchical role, the bearing of the burden of being the one professional agent of pastoral care, with sole prerogative in spiritual matters, leads increasingly in the single-handed modern parish, to a ministry that is entirely defensive. The clergyman finds he must put more and more energy into "stopping the wheels from stopping".'[4]

In addition to research projects into the church and local community—and learning how to handle these is vitally

[1] *Op. cit.*, pp. 51-2.
[2] Hodder 1964.
[3] *Op. cit.*, pp 85-107.
[4] *Op. cit.*, p. 12.

important—the student must be encouraged to work out some end-products starting from the basic material he is handling. A television epilogue, a youth-club talk, a programme for a young people's weekend, a dialogue sermon and an outline for a church membership course might be produced and evaluated by individuals or groups. If we are discussing the use of films in communication, it is not enough to show men how to work a projector. They must discuss religious and secular films and ask whether many points are not better made with the latter. For some people it will be relevant to go into the business of film-making, and so on. Within the overall dimensions of a term's course there must be considerable flexibility about the programme followed by individuals and full use made of experts from outside as well as of the expertise possessed within the college community.

Universities or Seminaries?

One of the fundamental dilemmas affecting discussion on theological training today is whether to concentrate it on the university faculties of theology which are obviously running well under potential or whether to continue independently with theological colleges which still offer a complete training, both academic and pastoral. The present Dean of York, Dr Alan Richardson and Bishop F. R. Barry, formerly of Southwell, have been outspoken in urging the Church of England to go back to the Universities. They feel that in an age of increasing specialization and the dramatic expansion of higher education, the Church will become even more marginal than it already is if ordinands do not receive the most rigorous academic training available and if theology does not make its pressure felt in the university community. There are many who rightly deplore the ghetto-like atmosphere of so many theological colleges which a member of SCM staff recently described as 'too cut off for comfort'. However, it is sometimes assumed that it is geography which isolates colleges and encourages the 'clerical tone' which laymen find so distasteful. Yet there are colleges way out in the country, such as the Seminary of the Mission de France at Pontigny, or distant from a university such as William Temple College at Rugby, whose intellectual standards and engaged position are beyond question. Meanwhile there are colleges in university cities which seem to belong emotionally to the Middle Ages.

If the contention is correct that the way in which the traditional matter is imparted is crucial, then it is clear that university degree courses are irrelevant. They are concerned with academic matter which can be objectively tested, not with communication, relevance or pastoral implications. There is little place in a university course for the kind of staff/student discussion about the contemporary world and the Church within it which is essential in *training for the ministry*. This really is the main purpose of the theological college community. It must be a community where worship and pastoral care have a high priority for their own sakes but where they coalesce with the process of learning and discovery that is taking place. If ordinands are to be asked to do more thinking and experimenting than previously, they must have the security of a free and voluntarily accepted community. Various estimates are given for the maximum number of a real community—300, 153, 90, 60 and so on. It is obvious that a college of around 100 is needed for economic reasons and there is no reason why colleges should not be larger provided that there is the opportunity for breakdown into smaller groupings. It is pious nonsense to suppose that any individual gets to know more than five or six of his fellows really well.

This is not to say that theology has no place as either an independent or ancillary discipline in the University.[1] It has, and those who want to pursue theology academically should be encouraged to do so. This will include many of those who will later teach in theological and training colleges—and

[1]But surely those who are pleading for more faculties of theology particularly in the new Universities must recognize that there is quite insufficient student demand.

laymen too. We need to get away from the idea that the only purpose for reading theology is to get ordained. At a recent SCM conference a woman student asked if I could recommend her a faculty of theology in England where she could study theology in the light of the secularization discussion. When I asked her why she wanted to read theology she replied, 'Because I'm interested in it.' Thank God! Dr Richardson's complaint that the system of theological colleges and first curacy or congregation cuts ordinands right out of the university world, is true given the current values of that world. Men are not able to spend two years after their first degree grubbing around in other people's books to produce Ph.D's of standard thickness. Why must the research degree—so often little more than hack work—and keeping up with all the articles in the ever-growing number of academic journals, be essential for university teaching? If the faculties want good men who haven't conformed to current academic orthodoxy they are quite free to revise their values.

Ecumenical Training

In a volume such as this in which writers representing three main traditions of British churchmanship have shared, it would be a serious omission not to deal with the imperative need for an ecumenical approach to the whole question of training for the ministry. This I do with profoundest conviction. It is surely impossible to train men to minister in 'the whole Church bringing the whole gospel to the whole world',[1] on a narrowly denominational basis. At Lund the Churches asked 'whether they should not act together in all matters except those in which deep differences of conviction compel them to act separately?'[2] To continue into an indefinite future training in independent denominational seminaries which condition men heavily against the goals of understanding, growing together and visible unity,

[1]Prof. J. C. Hoekendijk's definition of 'ecumenical'.
[2]Message of the World Faith and Order Conference, 1952.

implies a negative answer. We are in danger of paying lip-service to ecumenical resolutions. The fact that after 50 years of ecumenical work in this country we have not one united interconfessional theological college is a sad reflection on our integrity.[1]

Much progress has of course been made. The way in which biblical scholarship has developed makes it inevitable that the commentaries students use scarcely betray a denominational origin. The same goes for the lectures given in university faculties and there is a very considerable degree of consultation and joint planning of courses by college lecturers who are also on a faculty board. This certainly happens in Bristol, London, Birmingham, Manchester and Cardiff and probably in other places too. There is much less sharing of lectures between colleges as such where geography and accommodation present difficulties, but one may guess that co-operation is easier when neutral ground is involved.

Most colleges belong to some local association or union which links colleges of different denominations in a particular area. Theological College Unions of one kind or another exist at present in London, Cambridge, Oxford, Yorkshire, Manchester, Bristol and Ireland. They are student-organized bodies, in most cases independent of the SCM but often owing a good deal to the inspiration of an SCM Secretary for their origin. They vary immensely in their quality and if all were nearer what has been achieved in Cambridge the picture of inter-college involvement in England would be a lot brighter than it is. Cambridge, it must be admitted, is favoured by having five colleges representing four traditions, none of extreme churchmanship and all within a mile of each other. The TCU's activities there include hall-exchanges, residential exchanges, joint study groups, a termly service, annual residential and half-day conferences. A combined mission to Rugby took place in

[1]Students of several denominations participate in the excellent course at William Temple College but it is still an Anglican Foundation.

summer 1964 and Anglican and Methodists at least are sharing each others' hospital visitation and preaching. A tremendous encouragement to this programme is the fact that the principals meet once a term for dinner and discussion. It is not without significance that the Cambridge principals have requested the BCC Faith and Order Department to arrange a conference for theological college staff to consider how current ecumenical developments may be reflected in college curricula. It is hoped that this will be held in 1966. A number of residential exchanges are taking place on a somewhat sporadic basis in other parts of the country, for example between Spurgeon's and Lincoln, Headingley and Lincoln and St John's Durham and St Andrews. Yet it is disappointing to discover that one cannot trace any sort of growth in this pattern—things seem to be about the same now as they were ten years ago. The truth is that most colleges regard this kind of experience—living right inside another denominational tradition—as very much an optional extra for those interested, to be arranged when the stimulus comes from a student or some outside body or person. Given the obvious fact that denominational colleges are likely to be with us for some considerable time to come, one must plead that they become a mandatory feature of every student's course—as teaching weeks, industrial courses and missions or parish visits already are. The missionary situation in Britain make ecumenical strategy imperative and a man cannot be said to have been trained unless his eyes have been opened through experience to the genuine Christianity of his fellow Christians of other denominations. It is quite amazing to discover the myths which hold sway even in the minds of such educated beings as theological students. Many are ignorant of the most elementary facts about the faith and order of other traditions and have no feel for the values which others cherish.

This emphasis on experience over against teaching is deliberate, for all the academic teaching about Edinburgh 1910 and all that will fail to do what even a few hours' shared life can accomplish. At the same time there is a strong case for imparting information about some of the facts relating to the current ecumenical situation. This could be probably best done in the form of a case study, starting from a contemporary BCC or WCC Report, such as that on the British Nuclear Deterrent or the New Delhi declaration on unity. Only one or two colleges as far as I know have a specific course on ecumenical history, though it is interesting to note that Fr Bernard Leeming is giving such a course in a number of Roman Catholic seminaries in Britain. In the Faculté de Théologie Protestante in Paris. Professor Jean Bosc conducts an extremely valuable seminar series on ecumenical theology, examining the treatment of the main theological problems from a Protestant and Roman Catholic angle. In Berlin they had a seminar on the New Delhi documents as soon as they were published. I doubt if a dozen British theological students could offer more than the sketchiest resumé of New Delhi or name the main departments of the BCC. It is true that often the ecumenical organizations are not their own best publicity agents, but it is after all rather un-English to know too much about things centered on London or Geneva, especially when they are phrased in Americanese.

Here it may not be out of place to refer to the existence of the SCM Theological College Department which I now serve as secretary. This institution has been working among theological colleges on a fully ecumenical basis for 65 years and has numbered among its staff such distinguished figures as Leslie Hunter, Oliver Tomkins, Ambrose Reeves, Nicholas Zernov and Theodore Woods. It has organized national conferences at Swanick once every two years which have been attended by a large number of students from all parts of the British Isles and every denomination. Vacation job schemes in industry, conferences on Christianity and psychiatry, visits to and conferences with theological students of various European countries have been and are part of the programme in which we are engaged. The department's aim has always centred around a concern to be relevant to the needs of students in their preparation for the ministry in an ecumenical and missionary perspective. One of its great values has been to provide a link with students of other faculties through the life of the general SCM. One is aware that the name of SCM does not arouse enthusiasm or good-will in every breast but I would submit as a relatively objective judgment that only a very considerable degree of apathy is sufficient to explain the fact that many of the facilities we offer and have offered are not exploited to the full.

Indeed a statistical analysis would suggest a retrogression of ecumenical enthusiasm since the war. That this is not due solely to lack of imagination or diligence on the part of SCM may also be taken from the fact that still only about 18-20 students a year out of 700-800 in British theological colleges apply for WCC Scholarships to study abroad for a year in a college of another tradition. This year only two applied to go to the winter semester at Bossey—though the position is more encouraging for the three-week summer course.

But all this is merely tinkering with the problem. There is an urgent need in this country for a first-class union theological college, not just for the sake of the students who will go to it but for the great stimulus it could give to theological training in every tradition. There has been some talk of this in connection with the BCC Committee on Training for the Ministry but it is too early to know whether anything concrete will emerge. It is certain that theological colleges are not founded by vague talking but by determined men and women who have a vision of what needs to be done and will leave no stone unturned until their vision becomes reality. What a magnificent spur it would be to work for visible unity in this country if the BCC would set its hand to such a task. This would seal in hard fact the resolutions and covenants which have been so frequently made in the 21 years of its history. Is there not a danger of our practising the very kind of 'spiritual' unity which stops short of action involving organic change, which we are so quick to condemn on the part of certain evangelicals?

It would not be difficult to imagine the faculty of such a college and the opportunity for expertise it would provide. In size it would cater for 100-150 students and each denomination might close one of its smaller colleges to make way for it. A thoroughgoing theology of missionary strategy and experimentation would be vital. Though it could be tempting to make it a post-theological college concentrating on pastoralia it would be vastly preferable that it should offer total courses for the reasons previously stated. The rub would come at the point of residential accommodation and worship. If these could not be imaginatively and resourcefully faced and overcome, the college would be quite inadequate. The question of inter-communion would have to be faced—my only comment here is that the present *status quo* between the Churches is intolerable and that the eucharist should never be used to fortify or demonstrate a party position. The practice of dispensations and exceptions in Christian tradition might profitably be examined to discover a way through what is certainly an impossible, not to say blasphemous situation. To found a union college which does not provide a breakthrough in the whole approach to training would be a waste of effort.

Finally we must say a word about the discussion of secularization or radical theology which for some of us is so exciting and for others so distressing. It is clear that we are going to have more of it, especially since no objector can get round Bonhoeffer's point that modern man does not feel the need to resort to God as a working hypothesis. He does not feel lonely, alienated or guilty, and so all the ways of making him conscious of and obedient to God based on these analyses prove virtually useless. This cuts at the root of evangelism, apologetics, worship and dogmatics—though not of faith. Colleges must face up to this mood boldly and constructively and be places where students can live and think their faith out in a secular context. This means being acquainted with secular thought at first hand by lecture, discussion and reading, not knocking down aunt sallies put up by imaginary objectors. It means taking Sartre and Camus seriously, looking for the depth and truth of Christ—even if only partially expressed—in contemporary films, plays and novels. There can be little doubt that Christ is speaking to us from outside the Church today and we shall only be able to serve him through the Church if we are prepared to listen. This is not to suggest that the Church has no role but to listen. It is in the world to exemplify that community in which the love of Jesus is expressed in acceptance, forgiveness and self-sacrifice. Our training must give men the faith to come off the defensive and to be courageously open to life, as Jesus was. The fear that this means simply humanism is quite unjustified if the theological dimension of faith is preserved.[1] For the exposition of what I am trying to express here I would refer to the essay 'Jesus and Faith' in *Word and Faith* by Gerhard Ebeling.[2]

I have said little in this essay about the call to the ministry, deliberately. A shortage of candidates in recent years in some denominations is certainly causing deep concern to church leaders. In the past, vocation has been almost exclusively thought of as an inner psychological compulsion divinely activated by the Holy Spirit. Recently both writers[3] and responsible church organizations[4] have expressed the view that the Church may be responsible for stimulating the call as well as testing it. This is, after all, no more than a return to New Testament practice. May not this stimulus be most effective if men see that the Church is actively adapting its institutions and the presentation of its message

[1]As it does not seem to be by John Wren-Lewis in his talk' What are the Clergy for?' *The Listener*, March 1964.

[2]SCM Press, 1963.

[3]Victor de Waal in *Theology*, December 1962 and Basil Moss, *op. cit.*, pp. 33-34.

[4]CACTM has appointed a Recruitment Secretary; the Renewal Group has arranged unofficial conferences for potential Methodist candidates; the Congregational Union made a once-for-all appeal to local churches.

to the forms of contemporary society? Are there those in our Churches who are prepared to bring into existence one or more new colleges where men and women may be trained for a kind of pioneer ministry in renewal and communication? If there is sufficient conviction to do this I have little doubt that candidates of calibre will come forward and the 'powerful deterrents' referred to in the current CACTM Report[1] be met by a convincing challenge. It can still be as relevant to quit one's bench or one's desk today as it was for Peter, James and John to leave their nets in Galilee.

[1]*Men for the Ministry 1964* (Church Information Office).